BLACK POWER
FROM THE PEW

BLACK POWER FROM THE PEW

LAITY CONNECTING
CONGREGATIONS AND COMMUNITIES

STEPHEN C. RASOR &
CHRISTINE CHAPMAN

THE
PILGRIM
PRESS
Cleveland

The Pilgrim Press
700 Prospect Avenue
Cleveland, Ohio 44115–1100
thepilgrimpress.com

10 09 08 07   5 4 3 2 1

Library of Congress Cataloging-in-Publication Data
Rasor, Stephen Charles.
    Black power from the pew : laity connecting congregations and communities / Stephen C. Rasor and Christine Chapman.
        p.   cm.
    Includes bibliographical references.
    ISBN 978-0-8298-1751-5
    1. African Americans – Religion.   I. Chapman, Christine D., 1948-
II. Title.
    BR563.N4R325 2007
    277.3′08308996073 – dc22

                                                    2007000486

1 2 3 4 5 6 7 8 9 10   12 11 10 09 08 07

Contents

Preface   7

Introduction
Black Spiritual Power   11

Chapter One
Spiritual Power Connections   23

Chapter Two
Identity Connections   45

Chapter Three
Power Connections inside the Congregation   66

Chapter Four
Power Connections outside the Congregation   91

Chapter Five
Continuing the Journey   119

Conclusion   132

Appendixes   138

Notes   171

Preface

In the third chapter of John's Gospel, a Pharisee named Nicodemus visited Jesus one night. The Bible records a conversation between this "leader of the Jews" and Jesus. Nicodemus supposedly wanted to talk with Jesus because of the powerful "signs" that he had demonstrated. "Rabbi, we know that you are a teacher who has come from God" (John 3:2b NRSV). Jesus responded to him in a direct way, stating that a person must be "born from above" or "born anew" (NRSV) if he or she is going to see, or understand the meaning of, the reign of God. Nicodemus, as portrayed in John's Gospel, had difficulty understanding what Jesus was really talking about, especially the notion of being born again. Jesus tried to clarify the matter by explaining that God the Holy Spirit makes this happen in our lives, and we then see the results of the Spirit's activity in our subsequent behavior. "The wind [or Spirit] blows where it chooses, and you hear the sound of it, but you do not know where it comes from or where it goes. So it is with everyone who is born of the Spirit" (John 3:8 NRSV).

The power of God is most often witnessed in our actions. We don't always see the wind, or Spirit, but we see its effects. God initiates and controls God's power. As human beings we may confuse what is and what is not God's power, but more often than not we make fairly lucid observations about the results or effects of that holy power. Men and women who genuinely care for others, religious communities that embrace diversity and welcome "the stranger," people who work actively for economic and social justice, entrepreneurs who value employees as much as profit, families that model forgiveness and reconciliation — all illustrate the movement of the Spirit or the power of God in our individual and communal lives.

We have written this book because we have been overwhelmed by a great appreciation of black spiritual power. One of us has taught at the Interdenominational Theological Center (ITC), a consortium of six predominantly black Protestant seminaries, since 1984. Another one of us is a graduate of the ITC and also a sociologist of black religion. Together we have spent many years exploring the significant and unique aspects of African American congregational life using social scientific research methods to uncover those often neglected but important qualities of black spiritual power. Our hope is that African American local church leaders, both professional and lay, will use this book to better understand their church's strengths in ministry and mission. Another purpose for writing the text is to share our insights with denominational leadership in and beyond the black Protestant religious setting. Finally, we want students of religion and candidates for ministry to know the story of black spiritual power so that they will be better prepared for future ministry.

This book is a result of many people's hard work and commitment to the black church. The Lilly Endowment funded both of the major studies highlighted in the text — ITC Project 2000 and the Members Voice Project (MVP). Additional faculty members of the ITC Institute of Black Religious Life — Michael I. N. Dash, Marsha Snulligan Haney, and Edward Smith — made significant contributions to this endeavor. The MVP project was patterned after the U.S. Congregational Life Survey (US CLS), also funded by the Lilly Endowment, and directed by Cynthia Woolever and Deborah Bruce. Cecelia Dixon, Melody Berry, and others at the ITC gave their support and hard work to the project. More than one hundred ITC master's of divinity and doctor of ministry students helped with the survey. They opened many doors for us as we worked with local pastors around the country. We also thank Rev. Ernest Morris, an ITC 2006 graduate who facilitated the stories. Finally, the pastors, administrators, and laypersons among the four hundred black Protestant churches, fifty Catholic parishes, and twenty-six Muslim masjids we surveyed shared their churches' stories of ministry in their respective communities. While we are grateful to the numerous men and women who helped us complete the task and supported our purpose for writing it, we take full responsibility for the text. (See Appendix A: Research Methodology.)

The studies that support the primary claims of this book are the Members Voice Project (MVP)[1] and Project 2000,[2] but several other research endeavors have also been included: the Faith Communities Today Project (FACT),[3] the Institute of Church Administration and Management Study of Black Church Giving (ICAM),[4] the Institute of Black Religious Life (IBRL) Social Policy Survey,[5] and the U.S. Congregational Life Survey (US CLS).[6] The following table illustrates the variation among these different research endeavors, which are presented chronologically.

Project	Date	Purpose	Settings/Respondents	Director
ICAM	1998	Financing Black Churches	141 churches/ 3,637 worshipers and their pastors	Collier and Pressley
FACT	2001	U.S. Congregational Study	14,301 congregations/ pastors	Dudley and Roozen
Project 2000	2001	U.S. Black Congregational Study	1,863 churches/ pastors	Chapman, Dash, Rasor
IBRL Social Policies	2003	Black Church Leader Social and Public Policy Survey	200 pastors and seminarians	Chapman
US CLS	2002 2004	U.S. Congregational Study	2,000 congregations/ pastors and 350,000 worshipers	Woolever and Bruce
MVP	2005	U.S. Black Congregational Study	400 congregations/ pastors and 13,000 worshipers	Rasor and Chapman

The ICAM study sought to discover some of the keys to church giving among African American Protestants. Pastoral leaders and laity were questioned in urban and rural settings. Several important findings were discovered, some of which relate to spirituality, religiosity, and income. The study illustrated how some black church leaders effectively supported their local congregations financially.

The FACT project is the largest survey of congregations ever conducted in the United States. It is the most inclusive, denominationally sanctioned program of interfaith cooperation. Forty-one denominations and faith groups used a common core questionnaire covering six broad areas: worship and identity, location and facilities, internal and mission-oriented programs, leadership and organizational dynamics, participants, and finances. The pastoral leader was the primary survey respondent in the study.

Project 2000 was a significant part of the FACT program. The historically black denominations, ranging from African Methodist Episcopal (AME), Church of God in Christ (COGIC), and Baptist, among others, were included. The key respondent in the project was the local pastor. This national random sample of black congregations affirmed many of the strengths of African American churches, such as a strong commitment to community outreach, a deep sense of spiritual vitality, and an excitement about the future.

The IBRL Social Policy Survey questioned pastors and seminary students in the Southeast. The purpose of the survey was to have an initial examination of interest and current involvement in social and public policy issues. An important finding was the strong level of church leadership interest in social and public policy issues.

US CLS has focused mainly on the laity in American congregations. The people in the pew were given an opportunity to articulate their views on four key elements of congregational life: spirituality, internal church life, external activities, and congregational identity. While significantly diverse, the vast majority of lay respondents represented European American churches.

Finally, MVP, using most of the research questions developed through US CLS, focused exclusively on black Protestant congregations. The Protestant churches, approximately four hundred in number, were given our primary attention for this book. African American-populated Catholic and Muslim faith communities (forty-five Catholic and twenty-six Muslim) were also a part of the study but are not a concentration of this text. The black laymen and laywomen, as well as their pastors, were invited to share their views related to four building blocks of congregational vitality:

- ◆ Spiritual connections — understanding the many ways in which worship and faith are expressed within and throughout congregations

- ◆ Identity connections — identifying the various subgroups within congregations and how members view the future of their faith communities

- ◆ Inside connections — exploring worshipers' activities within the faith community and how these connections relate to one another

- ◆ Outside connections — assessing how congregations reach out to serve their communities

Both of us are grateful to members of our families, whose love and devotion we have especially valued: Susan and Joshua, Lee and Edgar (deceased) Rasor, Eleanor Rasor Appman (deceased); Margaret Meyer, Steve, Leah, Alianor, Max, Zack, and Delia Chapman.

Introduction

Black Spiritual Power

This book is about the power of God working in the lives of African American Christians in the twenty-first century. Black spiritual power has been and continues to be prevalent in and beyond African American church congregational life. There is power in the pulpit and power in the pews. Black pastors and African American parishioners consciously demonstrate their God-given power through their involvement within the church and the broader communities where they live. This text affirms black spiritual power and finds in it a great reservoir for community building, social change, and church development.

BLACK SPIRITUALITY

Black spiritual power is not necessarily the same general brand of spirituality thrust at us in many religious and social settings of the United States today. Many religious, social, and political enclaves use the word "spirituality" quite differently depending on the context, audience, or agenda. Bookstores have numerous books on their shelves describing myriad types of spirituality, which was not the case twenty years ago, but today, spirituality is in vogue and seems to sell — economically, socially, and psychologically.

In *Hidden Wholeness: An African American Spirituality for Individuals and Communities*, Michael I. N. Dash, Jonathan Jackson, and Stephen C. Rasor describe spirituality as a process that is experienced personally and collectively. It is personal, but not private. It involves groups of people and individuals. The experience of spirituality liberates human beings in a way that is both personally experienced and collectively grounded.

This liberating experience has three dynamic and interconnecting components. At one point is a liberating encounter, followed by a liberating reflection. In turn, we can experience a liberating action. This encounter, reflection and action can

11

penetrate and transform our individual and collective activity. We encounter God, because God intends that encounter. God is already active in the world, and we encounter God's presence. To be encountered by God is a liberating event, for God is the giver and sustainer of life.

Following that encounter, we experience a liberating reflection. That reflection can take many forms often associated with the so-called spiritual disciplines of prayer, meditation, scripture reading, storytelling, and worship. These disciplines provide a basis for the development of long-term spiritual formation. As we encounter God, the ground of our being, we are urged, impelled to do something in response. This in our Christian tradition often involves spiritually forming events, disciplines of the Spirit-prayer, sharing, worship, and service.

Finally, the encounter with God and the initial response to God arise out of God's initiative. The God whom we seek finds us. To be found of God is to experience a liberating encounter, whatever reflective form that encounter may take drives us outward and into the lives of others in the world in continual acts of self-giving. It is freeing when, as a result of the encounter/reflection, we are required to join God in God's liberating action in the social institutions and personal lives of God's people. Our spirituality is truly a liberating and whole one when we are compelled by the Creator and the creative energy of spiritual reflection to participate with God in the life-giving acts of justice and peace in God's world.

Thus, spirituality can result in liberation: a liberating encounter, a liberating reflection and a liberating action. Ours is a God who initiates this liberation from within the center of our being (the individual) and in the midst of our everyday activity (the collective) in the world. This liberating spirituality, we contend, is the key to our discovery of a hidden wholeness.[7]

Dash, Jackson, and Rasor argue that this particular form of spirituality has its roots in African and African American history, heritage, and journey. They suggest that spirituality in Western culture has often been overly associated with more private forms of religiosity (such as private prayer) as distinct from the public acts (such as community service) of faith followers. Many of our European American religious communities have reinforced this demarcation between public and private spirituality and thus constrained a more unifying and holistic spirituality. Black spiritual power gives more expansive meaning to the term "spirituality," speaking of a spirituality that is dynamic and cyclical in nature and suggesting a reality that is whole and embracing, not divided and alienated.

One result of this type of spirituality is the ease with which many members of black churches maintain both their deep personal involvement in their religious communities, while at the same time upholding commitments to social and political change. For black congregants, personal and public forms of spirituality are one and the same. One prays for God's presence and God's justice in the world. God's power is celebrated in prayer, worship, and Bible study. God's power is experienced in voting and challenging societal sins in public. Black spiritual power has been and continues to be present in personal and public discourse and actions. This book will demonstrate that reality.

The word "power" can be understood and advanced in many ways. Those of us who are active participants in the church have been exposed to sermons, Bible studies, and other adult learning settings wherein we heard and reflected on its meaning. We have explored biblical representations of power — God's power, the power of Jesus, and the power of the Holy Spirit. Some of us have pondered the use of power in and beyond the African American community in the past and at present. The civil rights era helped birth a new and energizing black power. We regularly discuss economic and political power in our private and public gatherings, especially through the lenses of various media. Finally, the church has on several occasions used moral and political power to advance the work of the reign of God.

The word for power in Hebrew is *kōah*. It suggests strength, force, or the ability to do something. Certain individuals, such as Samson and Daniel, are described as having special abilities. God is depicted in the Hebrew text as demonstrating strength or power. God cares for the people of Israel and uses God's force to help them. In the New Testament the word for power is seen as a noun and a verb. For example, *exousia* (noun) suggests freedom of action or the right to act, where *exousiazō* (verb) denotes the exercising of authority. The subject of power in the Bible, whether in reference to God, Jesus, the Holy Spirit, the angels, or human beings, is a very important one. God is powerful, and God uses that power absolutely

and without restriction. God gives power to others and thereby enables them to exercise that power. It has been said that "power" in
the Hebrew Scriptures and the New Testament may be categorized
in the following way: "(a) its original source in the Persons of the
Godhead; (b) its exercise by God in creation, its preservation, and
its government; (c) special manifestations of divine 'power,' past,
present, and future; (d) 'power' existing in created beings other than
humankind and in inanimate nature; (e) power committed to [hu-
mans] and misused by [humans]; and (f) power committed to those
who, on becoming believers, were empowered by the Spirit of God,
are indwelt by [God], and will exercise it hereafter for God's glory."[8]

In the Judeo-Christian tradition, women and men of faith have
attempted to understand and experience God's power. In the formation and affirmation of Scripture, they have claimed to experience
personal and collective forms of power. They have been empowered
to celebrate God, follow Jesus, and attempt to live under the guidance of the Holy Spirit. Many wonderful things have happened as
a result of these spiritual encounters. At times in history, men and
women have lived together in faithful pursuit of God and God's
reign. Jesus described a Christ-centered community in Matthew's
Gospel during what we call the Sermon on the Mount (Matt. 5:1–
7:48). In the early chapters of the Acts of the Apostles we witness
a community of disciples who earnestly desired to ground their beliefs and actions in the risen Lord. The epistles illustrate the early
church's challenge to be faithful and live in proper relationship to
God in Jesus Christ.

Early church fathers and mothers left examples for us of how one
respects the power of God and attempts to convey it. Many people's
legacies point to the existence of God's power through the ages —
Augustine, Martin Luther, John Wesley, Sojourner Truth, Richard
Allen, Ella Baker, Henry McNeal Turner, Martin Luther King Jr.,
and others. One can think also of the rural and urban churches of
America in which girls and boys grew to adulthood and learned
God's plan for their lives. The hospitals, colleges, and universities
that have come into being and continue to educate women and men
for the common good; the people clothed, children fed, prisoners
cared for — all of these transformative events happened because
God has throughout our history chosen to be with us and empower
us to do good in God's name. Much of our history since the birth,
death, and resurrection of Jesus can be seen as a series of interconnected events wherein God actively helps God's creation to grow
and flourish.

Human beings, however, have too often chosen to ignore God's available power and have even worked against it. While created to build community, we have worked at times to destroy it. Although God may have intended for people to love one another and show continuous acts of kindness, we have much too often found devious ways of hurting and killing one another. The creativity of the human spirit has at times been used in the worst possible ways to engender slavery, genocide, racism, sexism, economic exploitation, xenophobia, and other cruelties. We have misused the power that God intended to be used for good.

Individuals, groups, and nations have fought in the past and still fight today to exercise their power for evil. Instead of opening ourselves up to a God who created the world and its people to live in communion and peace, we choose the easier route of warfare and destruction. We give in to our fears and hatred and ignore the power of community building and reconciliation. Yet there have been times when we have overcome our tendency to crush one another. There will be times in the future when we will hopefully work harder at discovering and sustaining peace instead of relapsing into warfare and annihilation, but living in the Spirit and relinquishing our selfish desires and collective blindness do not appear to come easily for us. God created us for good, but we must still choose the good over the evil. God provided the earth and its many resources, but we must desire to share them. God appears to be always ready to help us find the better way, the alternative, and the path of Jesus. We have to stay on the path however, and time and time again, we have not done so.

The history of African and African American people, particularly over the past five hundred years, is a story of oppression caused by the abuses of power by European American peoples. They may have claimed to have the power of God but obviously were blind to and ignorant of that power and thus often misused it. To even suggest that God had anything to do with slavery, colonization, lynching, and political and economic disenfranchisement of black people, as European Americans have done, is to commit blasphemy. These terrible acts are stark opposites of God's plan for humanity. Racism and discrimination have nothing to do with God. Prejudice and exploitation are not of the Spirit. Jesus Christ was not Lord of a church that prayed and sang of salvation while enslaving and dehumanizing another race of people. Anyone who would suggest that these past five hundred years had anything to do with God's overall plan for humankind must not be taken seriously. Our biblical grounding, healthy theological interpretation, and well-informed ecclesiastical traditions would suggest that God wants us to enjoy God's power for the common good.

The genius of the women and men who led during the civil rights era — the Fannie Lou Hammers and Martin Luther Kings — is that they used our Judeo-Christian ideals of God's power and activity to call into question America's race laws and unjust treatment of people of color. In their various ways, Stokely Carmichael, H. Rap Brown, Angela Davis, Malcolm X, and others called for radical social change, asserting that all people were created equal and that God's so-called blessing of America was one that should be made manifest in human actions. They demanded an end to slavery and Jim Crow laws, separate but equal schools, poll taxes, redlined districts, and the like. They contended that we were either who we said we were — a nation underpinned by Judeo-Christian precepts — or we were living a lie. The civil rights era reaffirmed God-given "Black Power" and excluded any kind of power that would attempt to tear others down. One cannot fully understand and appreciate the multilayered complexity of the civil rights era unless one recognizes that the power being reclaimed in that period was a spiritual power granted by God and that this spiritual power was not always docile. It was power that pushed children and adults into the streets of America. It unleashed angry dogs and water hoses used against God's children. Churches were burned, children and grownups were killed. Older folks were placed in jail along with young people. People prayed, however, and pastors gave sermons, and African American people exercised their power. They sang about the blood of Jesus and shed their blood in the communities of our country. There is "power in the blood," power that God intended to be used for the creation and re-creation of God's reign on earth. The civil rights era was a significant time in the history of this country where we all were reminded that power can be destructive and that power can also be used to get us back on the proper path. Our God has always been with us, even when we have radically wavered from God's planned journey. James Weldon Johnson in his *Lift Every Voice and Sing* hymnal described the journey:

> God of our weary years, God of our silent tears,
> Thou who hast brought us thus far on the way,
> Thou who hast by Thy might, led us into the light,
> Keep us forever in the path, we pray. (1927)

MORALITY OF POWER

In 1977, Charles R. McCollough wrote a notebook on Christian education for social change. The title of the book is *Morality of Power,* and it was written to empower churches to bring about social change in American society. McCollough argued that individuals and groups need to consider three steps for fostering change. He suggested that grasping the social context of a situation or social problem was the first important step. People who don't like "the way things are" need to first be clear about the reality of the way things are perceived. Assumptions and perceptions may not be accurate and need to be critically questioned. Second, McCollough proposed that churches or individuals who want to participate in significant transformation need to envision alternatives for the future. It is not enough to grasp the reality of the problem; one must identify an alternative. Finally, McCollough submits the idea that churches need to use power to bring about change. Individuals, churches, and groups of churches have power and must use it to help society change. Poverty, hunger, institutional forms of racism and sexism, and other deep-seated societal woes will not be altered unless people of faith choose to participate in political and economic means of change. Spiritual people have power, which, when used appropriately, can effect change.

McCollough also recognized that effective and long-lasting social change requires several dimensions of growth or transformation. For systems and people to change, attitudes need to be altered. New knowledge needs to be shared and accepted. Skills that lead to behavioral change need to be developed. Finally, priorities must be defined or redefined. In other words, public and private awareness, analysis, action, reflection, and decision making regarding the changes required must provide the foundation for long-term social transformation. McCollough argues that the church of Jesus Christ can use its God-given power to create a more just and healthy society and world.[9] McCollough invites the church to cooperate with God as God redeems God's people. McCollough suggests that when used in appropriate ways, moral and political power can provide effective means for positive social change and global justice for all peoples. On the flip side, their distortion does not promote social justice, economic fairness, and political accessibility. Too often, power politics has a goal of power as an end in itself, while moralistic power advances an observance of a personal moral code narrowly defined by a particular group of people: "the righteous." Those who benefit from moral power include the have-nots and then the haves, while certain political constituencies benefit from political power. The haves seem to benefit most from power politics.

Decision makers differ in terms of how they use power: those in authority (moralistic), those most affected (moral), those who represent others (political), and those who have political power (power politics). McCollough suggests that the application of Scripture will even vary significantly depending on the type of power being employed: those engaging in power politics will consider the Bible as being irrelevant; political power mongers may pick and choose texts that seem to support their preferred government structures. Those employing moral power will often look to the life of Jesus to find support for a radical but nonviolent redistribution of power, wealth, and status. Moralistic power will selectively use Scripture to legitimize a particular and often biased viewpoint.

Finally, McCollough argues that people of faith should avoid the typical tactics exercised by those demanding moralistic power (a certain political or economic agenda cloaked in religious jargon) and power politics (using social control mechanisms to oppress and dominate). Instead he argues in favor of less threatening methods of resistance such as protest, persuasion, noncooperation and intervention (moral power), and the ongoing exercise of constitutional rights and justice (political power).[10]

All churches, including the black church, have used power in the past to advance their causes. All religious groups, including individual African American faith communities, have probably attempted to exercise all four types of power that McCollough describes. Most of us have observed local congregations, as well as national denominational bodies, that use moralistic power to argue for or against the ordination of women, the ordination of gay and lesbian persons, or the inerrancy of Scripture. Power politics, political power, and moral power have all been employed by pastoral leaders and faith communities to advocate for or against activities of war. Many black churches have demonstrated and continue to demonstrate power in the public realm in favor of their priorities. Not all black churches, are the same and certainly do not support the same causes or means of advocacy. One could make the case, however, and the data revealed in this text would support it, that many pastors who preach on Sunday and many laypersons who occupy the pews of black churches, believe God is active in their personal and communal lives and calls them into the world to exercise God's power. They encounter God's power, they reflect on that power, and they stand ready to advance God's will in their families, businesses, schools, and civic life. For many years, African American churches have worked to connect activities that happen within the church with those that happen outside the walls.

Black spiritual power is not a private, Sunday thing. It is a Monday and Tuesday thing. Black spiritual power is personal and social. It is for individuals and for the group. It is the result of God's hand in all phases of life. Life is interconnected, not segmented. Black spiritual power is relevant, forceful, and convincing. It has enabled a people of color to survive and thrive in a society and world that has more than once attempted to deny their rights or annihilate them. It is a spiritual reality instituted by God, modeled by Jesus, and sustained by the Holy Spirit. The connectedness evident in black congregational life bears witness to this truth.

CONNECTEDNESS

This book is fundamentally about the power of connectedness. One central and undeniable characteristic of black religious life is the deep sense of community witnessed therein. There is power in numbers, but especially in numbers of people who are bound through shared history, legacy, social reality, and common goals — and above all through a common faith. This in no way suggests that the black church in general or African American members in particular are a monolithic whole, but one cannot ignore the fact that the black church emerged out of, and in spite of slavery. Black church members have had multiple and varied life experiences but share a fairly common consciousness of America's racist institutions and systems.

Race does matter in the United States. It has mattered for a long time. It does not define all race relations, but it is a major factor. One of the strengths of the African American church has been its ability to witness to a God who liberates in the midst of enslavement, a God who dries tears of sorrow and gives tears of joy in the midst of oppression and pain, a God who cares for the marginalized and maligned, a God who gives purpose and power to those at the point of giving up. The black church provides an environment where African American people connect with God through Jesus Christ and, through the power of the Holy Spirit, transcend the limitations ascribed to them.

These churches are not all the same. Some churches "do church" or "have church" better than others. If one looks closely, however, one can see something unique in the black congregational experience. One can see a spiritual connectedness, a connectedness grounded in a common identity, an inside connectedness, and an outside connectedness.

PLAN OF THE BOOK

The following chapters investigate black spiritual power from the pulpit and the pews. We will demonstrate that African American Protestant churches do have power and that they use it within and beyond their walls. Drawing on the findings of the MVP study and Project 2000, each chapter will illustrate the God-given power expressed by men and women who support their local congregation. Through this text, we will let more than thirteen thousand laypersons voice their appreciation for and commitment to black Protestant congregational life.

The pastors of approximately nineteen hundred African American churches will also articulate their rich experiences in leading their respective faith communities (Project 2000). You will hear their voices and see some of their ongoing activities, their sense of purpose and vitality they express. You will be able to celebrate their commitment to social outreach and community service.

We invite you to consider the spiritual power demonstrated in this book. We attempt to clarify this power as we examine spiritual power connections (chapter 1), identity power connections (chapter 2), inside power connections (chapter 3), and outside power connections (chapter 4). Chapter 1 illustrates some of the ways laity and pastoral leaders participate in and direct spiritual practices. Chapter 2 demonstrates the sense of identity black church people feel related to their individual and collective characteristics and values. Chapter 3 highlights some of the ways worshipers and leaders are connected to one another inside their respective faith communities. Chapter 4 shows congregations' connections to the broader community. Each chapter introduces these various connections of congregational life and suggests a biblical foundation for that component. Personal stories of church members are given (names are changed). Key elements or concepts are explored, including suggestions for increasing organizational capacity within congregational life. Group exercises and relevant reflection questions re provided. The final chapter provides resources for using the book in your ministry setting. Our hope is that you will utilize the insights in this book within your congregational settings. Although the language of the book reflects an African American experience, the insights regarding the variety of spiritual power connections found within congregations can be applied to all congregations, regardless of culture.

STEVEN

The idea of community in the black church is one that has historical significance to many African Americans. The bonds forged within the church have held many communities together. Not only are families raised and maintained though the ministries of the church, but friendships are also established and strengthened.

Steven is a prime example of how the church can impact one's life. At age thirty-one he speaks of how the church has played a key role in the development of a nurturing, lifelong friendship. Coming to his church as a young adolescent (admittedly, because of his parents he had little choice in the matter) Steven found that one of the ways to make it fun was to find a group of kids to hook up with. He was lucky, because this particular congregation had a number of young people his age, many of whom had similar interests. There was one person he came to view as a brother; he, too, was always there because of the role his parents played in the ministry. Steven remembers his first meeting with this boy, who at the time was about twelve years old. He happened to be ushering at the time Steven's family was first visiting the church.

Steven's father is in a wheelchair, and sometimes people look at him as if he is not a real person. At times, even adults seem hesitant to approach him. This boy came right over, however, introduced himself, and welcomed Steven's family into the church without fear or hesitation. Impressed with this warm welcome, Steven learned that the boy also loved basketball, which immediately gave him two points! They started to hang out outside of church and began a friendship that continues on to this day.

Over the last seventeen years this young man has been a major part of Steven's life. This summer, he will stand up with Steven when he gets married, which means more to him than one can imagine. "We have seen each other through some difficult times, and I am honored to call him my friend," says Steven.

"I believe that the church is a place to not only find spiritual healing and support, but also a place where God places people in your life who can add tremendously to your existence. I believe that one of the only things you can truly pick for yourself in life is a friend, and through that bond you can grow as a person and as a community."

This brief story about Steven and his church relationships illustrates the power of congregational life and the deep connections black religious life can cultivate. Steven's story, similar to others provided in this book, gives a more intimate and personal feel for black power experienced in and beyond the church pew. Clarify how this story connects to the chapter, using words of "power" and "connection," with a brief introduction to the story.

Chapter One

Spiritual Power Connections

There is a balm in Gilead to make the wounded whole;
there is a balm in Gilead to heal the sin-sick soul.
                              — African American spiritual

Spirituality is at the heart of African American congregational life. Black men and women, boys and girls are connected to one another and the larger church community through spiritual power. The Holy Spirit is a force so necessary to church family life that one can hardly participate in worship or any spiritual activity without hearing the invocation for the presence of the Spirit. This is most evident in black religiosity among both pastors and active laity. Black Christians take it for granted that the Spirit is active and alive in the church body and the personal experiences of members. Religious life is a personal and social reality. Members are connected through the Spirit and enjoy that connection both in mind and practical living.

As we indicated in the previous chapter, spirituality is a hot topic for many authors and readers of religious materials. We are advancing a special kind of spirituality, however, one that contains three liberating aspects: an encounter, a reflection, and an action. We hold that the Creator is the holy one who initiates this spiritual liberation action from within the center of our being and in the midst of our daily activities. This spiritual liberation is experienced both individually and collectively.

God creates us as persons in community in such a way that we can experience ourselves, others and God in a liberating and open-ended fashion. As incredible as it might appear, African and African American men and women have held to this God in the midst of overwhelming suffering and pain. They have in the past and continue to forge a spirituality that could only be described as liberating. This spirituality has enabled many people of color to both claim their sorrow and express their joy.[11]

The liberating spirituality that drives African American religiosity is a powerful force. It can be demonstrated in people's stories as they testify of their profound encounter with God in the person of Jesus Christ, sustained by the Holy Spirit. This encounter is evidenced in the spiritual disciplines of prayer, meditation, Scripture reading, and worship. As African Americans encounter the Creator, the source of their being, they are impelled to do something in response. They tell their story and act on that story by serving others in the church and the community. Serving others (mission), celebrating God and God's people (worship), and growing in faith (education) are all significant and interlocking parts of the spiritual process. This powerful, sacred, and interconnected process links individuals and groups. The spirit of God is present as people serve God (action), worship God (reflection), and encounter God through service, worship, and everyday living. This spirituality does not divide people into body and spirit, private and public, encounter and action. It holds people together through the power of God's presence, which created humankind, sustains human activity, and beckons God's people into God's future and God's reign.

This chapter illustrates the various ways spiritual power has been demonstrated in African American churches across the United States. Adult members of black churches have indicated that they are serious about their personal devotion to God. They have stated clearly that they are growing in their faith as they participate in black congregational life. Their spiritual needs are being met, they enjoy and celebrate the Spirit in worship, and they adopt a variety of musical tastes. Their pastors describe their churches as being spiritually vital and vibrant. In addition, their clergy testify to diversity in activities and in music. These activities are grounded in a deep appreciation for scripture and the guidance of the Holy Spirit in interpreting the Bible for everyday life.

BIBLICAL FOUNDATION

Sometime later, I felt the Lord's power take control of me, and [God's] Spirit carried me to a valley full of bones. The Lord showed me all around, and everywhere I looked I saw bones that were dried out. [God)] said, "Ezekiel, son of man, can

these bones come back to life?" I replied, "Lord God, only
you can answer that," The Lord said:
    Ezekiel, the people of Israel are like dead bones. They com-
plain that they are dried up and that they have no hope for the
future. So tell them, "I, the Lord God, promise to open your
graves and set you free. I will bring you back to Israel, and
when that happens, you will realize that I am the Lord. My
Spirit will give you breath, and you will live again. I will bring
you home, and you will know that I have kept my promise. I,
the Lord, have spoken." (Ezekiel 37:1–3, 11–14 CEV)

Ezekiel was a prophet and priest. He was in Babylon like many
other Jews who had been exiled from Judah. God used Ezekiel to
preach the story of God's salvation to the Jewish captives, as well as
those still living in Jerusalem. He spoke of visions from God, warn-
ings from God, God's judgments on nearby nations, God's messages
of hope, and a vision of the new temple in Jerusalem. One of the
most memorable passages in the book of Ezekiel is his vision of the
valley of dried-out bones. The text testifies to the Lord's Spirit being
blown into the dead bodies and seeing them come back to life.

This passage, like others in the Bible, presents a story of God's
power and God's people that correlates with the spiritual journey
of Africans and African Americans. The blood and spirit of African
peoples had been drained from them during the agonizing period
of slavery in America. The U.S. laws and practices of segregation,
lynching, and dehumanizing acts attempted to produce lifeless and
spiritless men and women of color. Even today, overt and more
subtle acts of institutionalized racism can be seen as agents of death
and destruction. The biblical text in Ezekiel, however, declared that
God had something else in mind. God gave life back to those dry
bones. God breathed God's Spirit into what appeared to be lifeless
people.

In the face of the worst possible conditions, for hundreds of years,
people in Africa as well as African American women and men have
been able to grasp and be grasped by the Spirit of God, who made
a way out of no way. They have cried tears of anguish and joy
because the power of God was with them during the journey. The
spiritual journey has at many points been horrific, but the Holy
Spirit has sustained scores of African descendants as they sought
closer communion with the Spirit.

This text came alive for Stephen many years ago in the early
1970s. The Reverend Cecil Williams, pastor of Glide Memorial

United Methodist Church in San Francisco, preached in Atlanta, Georgia, before a mostly European American congregation. His charismatic and compelling style of preaching was fairly unfamiliar to that United Methodist congregation. He chose Ezekiel 37 as his text. As he preached, he walked down into the audience as if he were Ezekiel himself. The congregation experienced the power of this man, but more than that, they heard and felt the power of God in that large auditorium. Their bones stirred, and their spirits were moved. Bodies came alive. Differences of race, ethnicity, and gender were cast aside as they encountered the power of the Holy Spirit. God's story of liberation, Israel's story of liberation, and the story and journey of African and African American people all came together that day. Moreover, Glide Memorial Church in San Francisco is an example of God's power enlivening a congregation to serve its neighbors: It reaches out to the poor and the forgotten in the Tenderloin district. This church ministers to thousands of people by providing drug rehabilitation programs, food, shelter, and worship. Reverend Williams and his staff help to give new life to dying bodies every day. The words of the prophet Ezekiel are acted out in the Glide Memorial United Methodist Church. As this book shows, that is happening in many African American congregational settings.

KEY ELEMENTS FOR SPIRITUAL CONNECTIONS

Spiritual connections happen in a variety of ways in black congregational life. Individuals and groups devote themselves to prayer, meditation, and the reading of Scripture. They gather for worship on a regular basis. They enjoy enriching music. They hear sermons that give them specific, concrete, and practical ways to live in society and in the world. In the Project 2000 study, pastors highlighted sermon themes that addressed the spiritual needs of their parishioners: God's love and care, practical advice for daily living, and personal spiritual growth. The MVP study found laypersons confirmed that they felt empowered by these spiritual thematic worship experiences. As a result of these many religious experiences, they discover that many of their spiritual needs are met, they grow in their faith, and they profess to a vitality that they see in themselves and others. They are connected spiritually to God in Jesus Christ, to their extended church family, and to themselves. To say this in another way, devotion to God added to worship of God produces spiritual growth, growth in faith, and vitality in church congregations.

Private Devotions

Private devotional activities are an integral and important part of the faith journey. About 51 percent of the people surveyed in the Members Voices Project (MVP) spend time every day in private devotional activities (such as prayer, meditation, or reading the Bible). MVP African American worshipers are also more likely to spend time in these activities than worshipers surveyed in the U.S. Congregational Life Survey (US CLS), the largest and most representative profile of worshipers and their congregations ever developed in the United States. The national average of worshipers spending time in private devotional activities is 45 percent.

The personal dimension of religiosity is critical as individuals attempt to deal with the contingencies of everyday life. To be centered or grounded in one's faith is essential. The private devotional aspect of faith provides spiritual sustenance for work, family, and civic responsibilities. African Americans witness to their need for and commitment to periods of prayer, reading of Scripture, and studying religious periodicals and other materials as a way of preparing themselves for their more public life and daily activities.

Our study found the members of black Protestant churches quite clear about their priorities related to devotionalism and their awareness of how these religious practices have helped and will help them both cope with the stresses of life as well as make greater contributions in all areas of their life. They participate in personal and corporate experiences of devotion and worship, which influences their desire to share those experiences with others in and beyond their churches. Their journey inward relates to their journey outward. These life journeys are connected and therefore necessitate regular and consistent practice of devotional "holy" habits.

Listening to the individual stories of African American laity, one hears that the difficulty of living in a society that has not yet abandoned its racist and sexist dimensions necessitates the spiritual grounding of private prayer and Bible reading. This may suggest why black women and men appear to have always had this belief and found a way to act on that assumption: when life is tough, one can choose to double one's devotional grounding to prepare for and face head on whatever difficulty one may encounter. This admirable characteristic is available to all of us who profess our faith in God and God's activities in the world. Obviously none of us has reached

Private Devotions

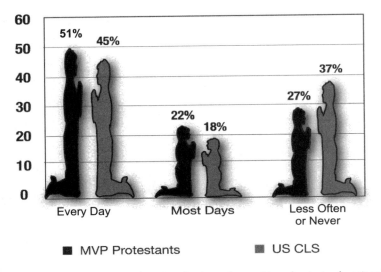

■ MVP Protestants   ■ US CLS

Spiritual connections are made primarily through worshipers' private devotional activities. About half of MVP Protestant worshipers spend time each day in private devotional activities (such as prayer, meditation, or reading the Bible), supporting the notion that African American worshipers are more likely to spend time participating in these activities as compared to US CLS worshipers across the country.

the stage of completion nor perfection in our ideational or behavioral aspects of religiosity, but when compared to some other laity in the United States some active black church folk know how the real world works and are committed to facing it with the assurance of private and personal spiritual centeredness.

CLIFF

Cliff has been the pastor of a northeastern urban church for thirty-six years and is actively engaged in many community and religious organizations. We discussed how much devotional time he spends with God, and how this has influenced his life — not only in ministry, but also in helping him teach his congregation about the benefit of living a life of personal devotion to God.

In 1979 Cliff's church was in the process of buying a new church building. The congregation had outgrown its current location and found an old computer manufacturing building that was up for sale. The building cost three hundred thousand dollars, which meant the church would have to take on a twenty-two-hundred-dollar monthly mortgage (after not having had a mortgage on their old building). Their electric bill of seventy-eight dollars a month would catapult to eighteen hundred dollars a month, and the building would need seventy-five thousand dollars of renovations.

"What does devotion mean to me?" repeats Cliff when we ask him. "First of all, a strong devotional life helps to build faith; it establishes a relationship between you and God. Devotion helps us to see the impossible, to have belief beyond our immediate circumstance. We teach that everything is possible with God. God is BIG and can move BIG."

"People ask how we can make this kind of move and where are we going to get the money," Cliff says. "I told them don't worry about what it looks like on paper. Trust that God will make a way. My faith comes from having a strong devotional life, and through that, an understanding of God's voice and instruction. Memory recalls what has happened, but imagination sees what has not come to pass. This is how I choose to lead my life — seeing what is ahead of me, and trusting that God is going to help me get there.

"In the black church, this is especially true. Why as a people have we not completely fallen apart? Why weren't we crushed completely? The answer is that some have been able to see the invisible, imagine the impossible, and, with the help of God, make the improbable a reality.

"A devotional life helps you to walk forward with hope and expectation. The relationship you establish with God enhances your quality of life. A life lived in devotion to God helps to ensure that your present conditions don't control you. With God, all things are possible and we were able to purchase the new building."

Worship Experiences

Worship in most religious communities is important but especially so in the Judeo-Christian tradition. African American laity treasure their collective experience of weekly worship. They articulate their personal and communal awareness of the centrality of worship and celebration. The people of God, gathered to praise God as well as support one another in the trials and tribulations of daily life, are foremost. Those who have reflected on the history and legacy of African Americans in this country point to the early activities of men and women who under the cloud of slavery, discrimination, and ongoing oppression found it essential to gather for collective strength and adoration of a God who helped them find a way to keep going. Public worship coupled with personal devotions brought a balance in a world that rarely supported that grounding. In fact, as one compares the experience of black adults with others in our American context, the tendency of a more individualist emphasis in the larger society appears to be less so among those in the African American religious context. Discovering and sustaining strength through connectedness in the worship of God is important for most all of those in the Christian community. The history and present reality of our American social, political, and economic environment, however, has helped some black congregation members to demonstrate their perceived need to gather for weekly worship.

EDDIE

Eddie is a forty-year-old father of three children. He is also an associate minister at his local church and has been involved in the ministry for eight years. We asked him about his ideas of worship and what worship means to him.

"Worship is for me an unselfish form of venerating the Lord. It is not asking anything for yourself, but it is just giving love to God. Worship comes from a relationship that one has with God; it is that thing that we as humans can do to show the ultimate form of appreciation and respect. Many times we do not allow ourselves to get lost in God enough to really worship in

Worship Experiences

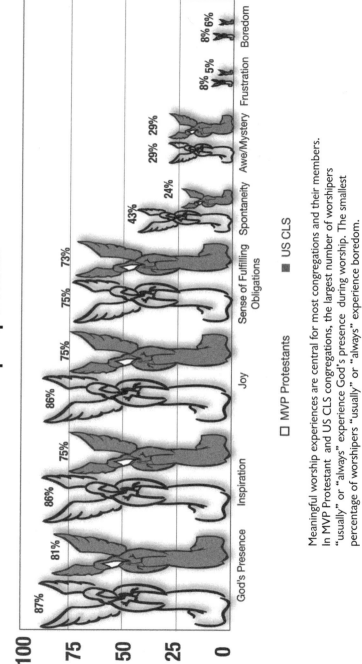

Meaningful worship experiences are central for most congregations and their members. In MVP Protestant and US CLS congregations, the largest number of worshipers "usually" or "always" experience God's presence during worship. The smallest percentage of worshipers "usually" or "always" experience boredom.

Legend:
□ MVP Protestants   ■ US CLS

Categories (left to right): God's Presence, Inspiration, Joy, Sense of Fulfilling Obligations, Spontaneity, Awe/Mystery, Frustration, Boredom

Values:
- God's Presence: 87%, 81%
- Inspiration: 86%, 75%
- Joy: 86%, 75%
- Sense of Fulfilling Obligations: 75%, 73%
- Spontaneity: 43%, 24%
- Awe/Mystery: 29%, 29%
- Frustration: 8%, 5%
- Boredom: 8%, 6%

church. We are often distracted by our neighbors or friends. Other times we can just get caught up in our own minds, and miss out on the blessing of worship. Worship is not bashful. We should not be ashamed to worship; it is reverent and truthful.

"Worship can be done on an individual basis or in a collective setting. It is a beautiful symphony when it is done in truth with other believers. Worship brings about change; there are times when the room seems to fill up with the presence of God because of the worship atmosphere. One misconception about worship is that one has to be in a church setting to worship. We can worship God in any setting. Worship can also come in different forms; it is not always oral, but it doesn't make it less genuine. There is one thing that is universal about worship, and that is that anyone may take part in it.

Making Music

Those who have studied the African American religious experience understand the music's importance, which can be traced back to the slave period. "Toward the end of the eighteenth century missionaries realized that the only way to succeed in converting the slaves to Christianity was through the use of music. They recognized that the African slaves were unwilling to give up their worldview and musical practices for Christianity. So they began to incorporate the musical practices of the slaves whenever they provided religious instruction, especially during worship."[12]

Any casual observer of the wide variety of musical expressions in African American churches will note that music is still a high priority. Music can be generated by an individual or group with or without instrumentation. The diversity in itself illustrates its importance. Personal and collective musical expression helps those gathered in community to enjoy and celebrate their faith in God. Music making makes for celebration, praise, and preparation for African Americans as they act out their beliefs and hopes for the present and future.

Black church folk in our study seemed to affirm a diversity of musical religious expression. They have in the past been forced, to some degree, to listen to and appreciate more European and traditional European American preferences in musical selection. They have and continue today to adapt and create their own unique music while affirming those traditions that seem applicable in their contemporary religious context. They celebrate the diversity of musical forms instead of being bound by only a select few.

Help With Everyday Living

The challenges of our personal and professional lives can limit our ability to engage in meaningful social interactions with family, friends, and coworkers. Unemployment, underemployment, marital strife and other family issues, medical problems, and financial woes all create stress and uncertainty that can upset our psycho-emotional equilibrium and undermine our faith. To what extent does congregational life help worshipers with the challenges of everyday living? Seventy percent of the black worshipers in the MVP study reported that they are helped with everyday living "to a great extent" by worship or congregational activities, compared with 45 percent of US CLS European American congregants.

SANDY

At times, our growth in faith seems almost like a contradiction, because more often than not, our growth is obtained through life's struggles. Yet through these very struggles we are able to testify to the power and victory that comes from transcending our hurdles to reach that higher ground.

Sandy's story centers on adversity and pain as a means to growth and victory, and how it has affected her life and ministry. A retired schoolteacher and mother secure in her middle-class existence, she has been involved in church ministry for a number of years, devoting her life to the work of God for the benefit of humanity.

"Growth in faith for me says that God has always been there, even when I've been down. Many people ask the question: 'Why is this happening to me?' Ultimately, the answer is 'to make you stronger.'"

What has been the most trying in Sandy's test of faith — as is the case for many women, particularly for African American women — is her marriage. Her marriage has been a test of her faith in God and God's word, yet through prayer and spending

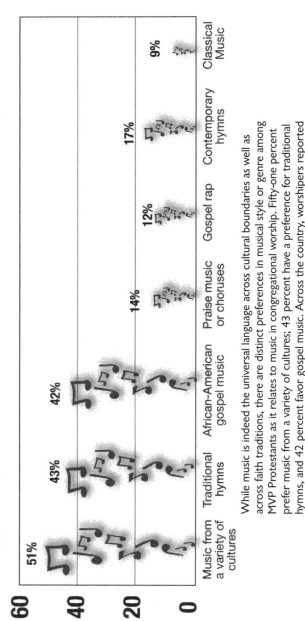

Types of Music Preferred in African American Churches

Music from a variety of cultures	Traditional hymns	African-American gospel music	Praise music or choruses	Gospel rap	Contemporary hymns	Classical Music
51%	43%	42%	14%	12%	17%	9%

While music is indeed the universal language across cultural boundaries as well as across faith traditions, there are distinct preferences in musical style or genre among MVP Protestants as it relates to music in congregational worship. Fifty-one percent prefer music from a variety of cultures; 43 percent have a preference for traditional hymns, and 42 percent favor gospel music. Across the country, worshipers reported the following preferences most often: traditional hymns (61 percent), praise music (33 percent), and contemporary hymns (25 percent).

Do Worship and Congregational Life Help with Everyday Living?

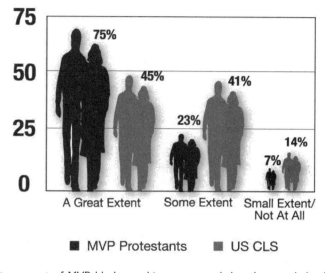

	A Great Extent	Some Extent	Small Extent/ Not At All

■ MVP Protestants   ■ US CLS

Seventy percent of MVP black worshipers reported that they are helped "to a great extent" by worship or congregational activities, compared to 45 percent of US CLS European American congregants.

time with God, she has risen above her problems—not only to survive, but also to transcend the challenges of her situation.

"When I look at growth," says Sandy, "I see in nature's plan that for things to grow, something usually has to die. For a plant to grow the seed must die. Sometimes for our faith to grow, we have to be tried and tested. It is not easy, and we make it through like Peter—on boards and broken pieces—but when we get to the other side, the reward is all the more meaningful."

Even in the Bible, the righteous suffered. When we consider Job, his suffering may seem unfair, but if we follow his story to the end, we see that he was ultimately given back far more than he lost.

Why do African American worshipers report they are helped "to a great extent" by worship or congregational activities compared to European Americans? What is unique about African American worship or African American family life that may support a need for "help with everyday life"? To frame our MVP findings, we present here portions of a report published by the Institute for American Values on the consequences of marriage for African Americans.[13]

In the last three decades, the proportion of African Americans who live in families where the parents are married has declined sharply. During the late nineteenth and early twentieth centuries, family formation patterns were relatively similar for African Americans and whites, with marriage occupying a paramount place in family life.

The twentieth century, however, saw a dramatic reduction in marriage rates among African Americans. Between 1950 and 1996, the percentage of African American families headed by married couples declined from 78 percent to 34 percent.[14] This trend was created by a growing divorce rate and, increasingly over time, a growing number of households headed by never-married African American women. Between 1950 and 1980, the proportion of African American households headed by never-married African American women increased from 3.87 to 69.77 per 1,000.[15] Not surprisingly, the decline in marriage rates among African Americans produced dramatic changes in the living arrangements of African American children. Between 1940 and 1990, the percentage of African American children living with both parents dropped from 75.8 percent to 33.2 percent — largely a result of marked increase in the number of never-married African American mothers.

Some scholars argue that declining marriage rates have contributed to the hardships that African Americans face. Researchers argue that father absence tends to create and perpetuate poverty and generally leaves children with a less-than-ideal starting point in life. There is an empirical basis for these claims. A study of approximately fifty-seven thousand households with children finds that marital status is a major determinant of poverty for African Americans. Another study finds that increased marriage rates would substantially reduce child poverty among African Americans in theory, and actually did significantly reduce child poverty during the 1990s.[16]

Other scholars have focused on understanding why marriage rates are low among African Americans and have noted that the practices of slavery, subsequent poverty, and discrimination, have cultivated conflictual gender relations and undermined the formation of stable, married families in the African American community.[17] Also a lack of economic opportunities for African American men has steadily reduced the number of marriageable African American men over the course of the twentieth century.[18]

Others argue that African American family structure represents a critical link in the chain between the structural disadvantage African Americans face and the generally poorer outcomes they experience. First articulated by W. E. B. DuBois in *The Negro American Family* (1908), this theory became both famous and infamous in 1965 as a result of the Moynihan Report, which argued that father absenteeism in the African American community — along with racism and unemployment — drives a "tangle of pathology" that conspires to keep African Americans from improving their circumstances.

Still other scholars have contested this position. They have argued that the single-parent, extended, and foster families more common among African Americans are not necessarily negative, and are in many ways positive: They reflect African cultural-familial norms[19] and have allowed African Americans to cope with the hardships they have faced in America.[20] Many of the same scholars argue that it is not so much family structure that is important for African American well-being as it is the quality of family interaction, socioeconomic status, and other factors.

We have chosen to use this framework for discussion of our MVP findings for several reasons. First, marriage promotes economic, social, familial, and psychological well-being for African American men and women. Second, in areas of delinquency, self-esteem, and school performance, having one's married father in the home appears to be a crucial determinant of better outcomes for young African American males at all stages of life. Last, marriage typically increases the income and economic situation of African American families; thus they are far less likely to live in poverty than other African American families. These three factors, as well as others, help frame an understanding of why African American families may experience extensive "help with everyday living" within their congregations.

Meeting Spiritual Needs

As a result of private devotions, weekly worship, good music, and help with everyday living, African American congregants find that their spiritual needs are being met. What we may want obviously may not be the same as what we need. Part of spiritual maturity is discerning the difference. Those individuals who gather as a spiritual community have the advantage of holding each other

Congregation Meets My Spiritual Needs

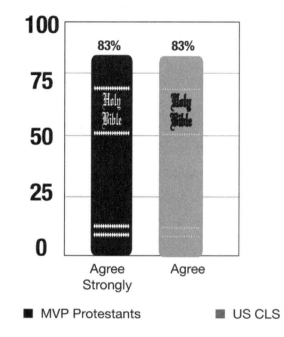

MVP Protestants   **US CLS**

What churchgoers seek can differ from denomination to denomination and from person to person. Most common among congregants is their need for spiritual fulfillment. Like the majority of worshipers across the United States, 83 percent of MVP Protestant worshipers feel their congregations meet their spiritual needs — the same percentage as that of worshipers across the United States.

---

accountable in this regard. Our collective understanding and interpretation of Scripture, tradition, reason, and experience can facilitate this discernment as we all struggle to follow the way of Christ and be exemplary disciples in God's world. A fundamental idea for most religious communities, one that is true for African American pastors and laity as well, is the assumption that our spiritual hunger and thirst for God's presence and direction is critical. It is certainly not "all about us," but our religious activities do support our personal and collective spiritual needs as we work and play in God's world.

Our research and personal awareness of black congregational life affirm that spiritual needs have to be addressed and celebrated to make church life vital. We participate in the mission and ministry of the church in such a way that while we serve we are in some important ways served by the Spirit. As we give ourselves away to responsibly respond to the needs of those both inside and outside our church doors, we discover that God is with us and that God cares for us and loves us. What a wonderful discovery. We participate with God as God feeds others. We in turn enjoy spiritual nourishment.

Growing in Faith

Congregational life is frequently cited as a key contributor to helping worshipers grow in their faith. Fifty percent of the worshipers in MVP congregations say their spiritual growth comes from their involvement in their congregations. About half of the people in American congregations (55 percent) and 75 percent of the people in African American churches surveyed MVP have experienced significant spiritual growth over the last few years, which is attributable to a variety of sources. Continuous participation in worship, exposure to deeper levels of Christian education, involvement in the decision making of congregational life, ongoing participation in social outreach and mission, as well as the other less visible but relevant forms of Christian character building all contribute to the growth of faith among black congregants and their leaders.

Most of us want to feel that we are moving closer to God, and the evidence of this study suggests that is happening in certain African American religious contexts today. However that growth is fueled — through more personal acts of piety or more public endeavors of mission and witness in the world — the respondents to our study of black spiritual power appear to be celebrating that growth.

Spiritually Vital Churches

The spiritual vitality of one's church appears to be a key contributor to its ability to meet spiritual needs and help parishioners grow in faith. Almost all leaders of black churches believe that their congregations are spiritually vital. Eighty-eight percent of all Project 2000 respondents (pastoral leaders) used "very well" and "quite well" to describe their churches' spiritual vitality. Obviously vitality can mean different things to different people depending on their worldview and context, but generally the perception and research among African American pastors, laity, and seminary students suggest that vitality has, at the very least, to do with experiencing an aliveness

Worshipers Growing in Faith

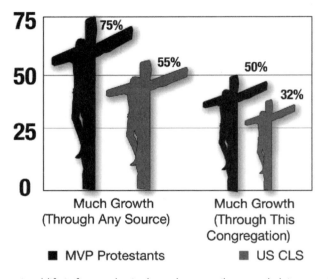

Congregational life is frequently cited as a key contributor to helping worshipers grow in their faith. While 75 percent of MVP Protestants report spiritual growth through a variety of sources, only 55 percent of US CLS congregants say they gain spiritual growth from all sources. Regarding spiritual growth that comes specifically from their own congregations, half of MVP Protestants report that their church experiences help them grow in faith, while only 32 percent of US CLS churchgoers report the same.

and relevance in and outside the church doors. To experience yourself and your congregation as being vital has something to do with sensing that one's beliefs and behavioral manifestations of those beliefs are generating self- and collective joy and sensitivity to God's presence and activity in God's world. To feel vital is to feel needed and joyous about that reality as we participate with God as God redeems God's creation. Being alive and relevant as we participate with God's mission and ministry is spiritually rewarding. Our study found that the pastors of black congregations across America feel spiritually rewarded by the vitality of their congregations.

Vitality is often demonstrated, according to the African American faithful we have been privileged to know and enjoy, in regular attendance at worship, greater financial support, and increased activity in and beyond the church as well as profession of growth in

Degree of Spiritual Vitality among Churches

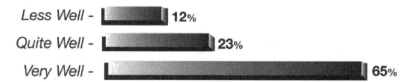

Less Well - ▐ 12%

Quite Well - ▐ 23%

Very Well - ▐ 65%

The vitality of a congregation, which is generated by pastors and lay church leaders, is crucial to the growth, if not the survival, of the church. It is the parishioners who support the mission, goals, and financial health of the church. Stagnant or declining membership can significantly diminish support on all levels. Almost all leaders of black churches believe the characteristics of being spiritually vital and alive describe their congregations.

---

faith, expressed and affirmed in numerous ways. Measuring more personal dimensions of religiosity, such as deeper feelings of security and certainty about God's presence, may be less obvious, but they also seem to illustrate degrees of evidence of assumed vitality. Our roles in an African American seminary setting as well as ongoing activity in the black church affirm these findings.

Spiritual power is what it suggests: powerful. This chapter has demonstrated the spiritual connectedness that African American laity and pastors articulate as they reflect on their awareness and celebration of those experiences within their religious communities. Private devotions, worship experiences, making music, discovering help with everyday living, meeting of spiritual needs, growth in faith, and personal and collective experience of vitality are the measured experiences of spiritual connection.

GROUP EXERCISES

The following exercises are brief spiritual connection exercises (one to two hours) that Sunday school or fellowship groups can utilize to begin examination of spiritual connections within your congregation.

Exercise 1: Analyzing Your Church's Spirituality

This exercise helps you explore some aspects of spirituality in your congregation. Spirituality points to a life of living in the Spirit, whereas spiritual formation refers to being nourished and sustained in such a life. All people have some sort of spirituality. Most people hold fast to something beyond themselves. We order our lives based on belief in some fundamental essence. At our core being, we love someone or something deeply. We live life, in part, grounded in that prior love. In the Judeo-Christian tradition we claim a "prior love" that is connected to the Spirit of God. Spirituality concerns our life in the spirit, and we participate in spiritual formation activities to nourish that life.

Examining all three of the following components of spiritual resources, as they are present in varying degrees within the congregation. Spirituality expresses itself through personal attributes of the church leadership and other members, the communal assets of the church leadership and members, and the outreach or community-centered activities of the church leadership and other members. People grow spiritually through both private and corporate activities. They pray by themselves and collectively in religious gatherings.

Each of the following topic areas could be a separate Sunday school or fellowship discussion.

Personal attributes

Identify the personal attributes of the church leadership and other members including their prayer life, Bible study, and perceived growth in faith.

- Where do we pray? How often? By ourselves? With others?
- How do we conduct Bible study?
- In what ways have we grown in our faith?
- How spiritually vital is our church?

Communal assets

Identify the communal assets of the church leadership and members, including their worship attendance, church school attendance, decision-making activity within the church, and public sharing of their experiences.

- How often do we attend corporate worship?
- How often do we participate in church school?
- What is our involvement in decision-making activities?
- Where and when do we freely share our spiritual life story(ies)?

Outreach activities

Identify the outreach or community-centered activities of the church leadership and other members, including their financial giving patterns, public witnessing, advocacy for justice, and actions to help others.

+ How much financial support do we provide to ministry and mission activities?
+ When and where do we witness to our faith in Christ?
+ How involved are we in advocating for justice in our society?
+ In what ways do we volunteer to help and serve others who need our help?

Exercise 2: Concerning the Whole Church

Church leaders and members demonstrate their spirituality through community outreach activities. Their spirituality will either lead them toward or away from various ethical, moral, and political decisions and behaviors. The greater the spiritual resources, the greater the impact that people and communities of faith will have on other individuals, families, and communities. Spiritual people and their churches exercise spiritual power for the common good in keeping with the will of God.

How can these spiritual resources be measured? Churches can determine how often and in what ways leaders and church members should uphold the personal attributes, communal assets, and resultant community activities of church life. The following questions encourage reflection on your congregation's spiritual resources to determine how your church's personal assets, communal assets, and community activities are being used as spiritual resources.

+ What is congregation-wide spiritual assessment, and why is it important? Define what your congregation's understanding is of a spiritual assessment based on this chapter's discussion of spiritual assessment and why a spiritual assessment is important for your congregation.
+ How does the congregation prioritize church programs?
+ Which care groups in the congregation promote supportive, open, healing, and trusting relationships with others?
+ How does our congregation welcome new parishioners?
+ What does social justice mean in the congregation and its community?

+ What are our assumptions regarding worship, liturgy, and music? What assumptions do church leaders make regarding worship practices, choices of liturgy, and types of music? Who makes the decisions regarding these matters? Try and identify particular assumptions church leaders make regarding worship, liturgy, and music.

+ What commitments are we willing to make, given who we are, what our strengths are, and what resources we can access? What commitments does our congregation make to its members? What commitments does our congregation make to the wider church community (i.e., our denominational connections)? What commitments does our congregation make related to special ministries in which we are engaged (i.e., a homeless ministry or a prison ministry)?

SPIRITUAL CONNECTION
REFLECTION QUESTIONS

1. What are some of the important beliefs, religious practices, and rituals that are distinctive to our denominational heritage and group identity?

2. How can we create a plan for a spiritual assessment of our congregation?

3. Why do our members care about the ministries in which they are involved?

4. How are children and youth cared for in our congregation?

5. How can we meet the needs of elderly people in the congregation and beyond?

6. What is the relationship between how well our members understand the church's mission (purpose) and their level of *participation* in church activities?

7. In what ways can our congregation imagine, plan, and develop strategies to assess its congregational life?

Chapter Two

Identity Connections

> We are climbing Jacob's ladder.
> We are climbing Jacob's ladder.
> We are climbing Jacob's ladder.
> Soldiers of the cross.
> — African American spiritual

In most cases, the identity of an individual develops over time. Churches are similar in that way. Over time, black churches create and re-create their own unique style and personality. The spiritual realities inside and outside their walls galvanize the formation of their identity. There is power in knowing who you are and acting accordingly. When a church puts its stamp on its members, their lives and their communities can be powerfully transformed. African-American people of faith carry the collective identity of their faith communities with them into their work, family life, service, and recreation. The need to be identified with a particular religious context is critical to black spirituality. The connectedness that underlies black spiritual power, both within and beyond gatherings of the faithful, draws from individuals' understanding of that collective identity. Identity is crucial to the effectiveness of ministry and mission in the world.

Nancy Ammerman, Jackson Carroll, Carl Dudley, and William McKinney, in their *Handbook for Congregational Studies,* define the "identity" of a congregation as the "persistent set of beliefs, values, patterns, symbols, stories, and style that makes a congregation distinctive." They suggest that "a congregation's identity is a result of the elaborate communication among its members through which they shape perception of themselves, their church, and the world — communities in which they develop and follow common values and by which they engage in corporate recollection, action, and anticipation. Identity changes over time but it mirrors a congregation's enduring culture."[21]

45

Understanding the identity of a local faith community is of vital importance to the clergy and lay leadership of a church. Helping churches expand their ministry can only be accomplished when congregations are clear about their identity and perform within that self-understanding. There are several key components of a church's identity:

- history
- heritage
- worldview
- symbols

- ritual
- demography
- character[22]

Most people know or want to know the *history* of a local church. Similar to the sense of identity gained from understanding the history of our nuclear and extended families, being able to recite and reclaim our church's history is part of what it means to be a member. The historical aspect of a congregation's identity also shapes the various expected futures the faith community anticipates.

Churches typically originate from a particular *heritage*. Being a part of, say, the African Methodist Episcopal denomination or other faith tradition is a significant part of a church's identity. Church members who have been identified with that tradition for a period of time are often proud of their heritage and try to assume the markers of that identity. Individual churches claim their "great traditions" as, say, members of the Church of God in Christ. Their social context, history, demographics, leadership, and other factors may be localized, but yet they adhere to the identities of the larger national denominational bodies. Being a Baptist church differs from being a Christian Methodist Episcopal church, but both types of polity have both localized and more corporate elements of tradition.

Churches have leaders and active members who see things certain ways. They attempt to explain what they perceive within the framework of their *worldviews*. Many things help to shape the ways we see the world, particularly the ways we have been socially conditioned. In other words, a well-educated middle-class man will often see the world differently than a less educated unemployed single mother. All of us are influenced by our socioeconomic status and often perceive and explain reality, in part, based on our social conditioning. Our theological mind-set can be influenced by the way in which we view our world and its inhabitants. Often, people with similar worldviews will often gravitate toward congregational settings that appear to have like-minded individuals and groups. We tend to stay with others who believe the same things we do. Individuals certainly differ, and every church, large or small, attracts people with differing worldviews. When congregational leaders take the time to dig beneath the dominant worldviews held in a congregational setting, however, they will discover another layer of the church's identity.

Symbols, or objects and actions that convey multiple meanings, are another important ingredient in the local church's identity. Some symbols are fairly traditional and obvious, such as pictures, crosses, steeples, or a building. Some are less obvious representations of often subconscious assumptions and stereotypes, such as the skin tone of Jesus in pictures, or the gender group that always receives the task of cleaning up the kitchen. All of us operate within symbolic systems. Often, key symbols convey meanings that frame parts of our identity as a church.

Rituals are also important to consider when we are trying to better understand congregational identity. Rituals are repetitive actions that reinforce meaning. Having an annual revival or barbecue is a ritual. Baptizing a baby or an adult is also a ritual. Where people sit and where it is assumed that some people should not sit are part of our rituals. The assumed patterns of behavior preceding and following a funeral of a longtime church member are ritual events. We often follow these patterns of behavior without ever reflecting on why we do so. It is a part of what we do and who we are — our identity.

The attributes of church members and attendees in a particular location constitute the *demography* of a faith community. The makeup of a congregation in terms of age, sex, marital status, race, ethnicity, and so on is all part of a church's identity. Where churches are located and how they relate to their surrounding neighborhoods and broader communities often are influenced by the kinds of people who live in that locale — whether they attend church, how much money they give, and so forth. Knowing the demographic characteristics of those in surrounding areas is important for a congregation's understanding of its identity.

Finally, the personality of the collective group that actively supports the local church is the *character* of the church. The unique dispositions and traits of a faith community are part of a congregation's character or overall identity. Church members often make individual and group decisions based in part on their ethos or sense of values. What is deemed as appropriate and at times inappropriate is determined by the unique moral identity of each church's congregation. When church bodies are experiencing a period of crisis or threat, they often assume or attempt to articulate a set of moral boundaries that will supposedly help them work their way through the difficult times. Obviously, problems can get worse when not all leaders or decision makers agree on those moral boundaries. Conflict can and often does arise. Pastors and lay leaders who have a fairly clear sense of the character or personality of a congregation can help steer the mission and ministry of the church during rocky periods.

Understanding the identity of a particular religious body is important for several reasons. This chapter illustrates some of the various ways that identity has been demonstrated in African American churches across the United States. These churches vary in size and location. Their demographic profiles in terms of gender, age, education, and household composition are also diverse. The women and men who are active in these congregations are open to change and new directions. They claim to have a clear sense of vision, goals, or direction as they execute mission and ministry. They state unequivocally that they highly value preaching, Bible study, and other ingredients of their congregational life.

BIBLICAL FOUNDATION

But you are a chosen race, a royal priesthood, a holy nation, God's own people, in order that you may proclaim the mighty acts of [God] who called you out of darkness into [God's] marvelous light. Once you were not a people, but now you are God's people; once you had not received mercy, but now you have received mercy. — 1 Peter 2:9–10 NRSV

The adults and children who have responded to God's call are special — a chosen people. Whether we are considering those early disciples of Christ, early congregations organized by Paul and others, or the faithful followers in Roman Catholicism and the Protestant traditions, people who have affirmed their claim by God in Jesus Christ are special. The words of Peter's first letter make that clear. God intended for humankind and God's gathered community to celebrate their special place and status: "A chosen race, a royal priesthood, a holy nation" — not for a position of privilege but as a special responsibility. God does the calling. God makes the selection, and those who hear the calling and claim the place of responsibility are those who are God's own people. With this anointing comes great responsibility and sacrifice, but the starting point is with God. Jesus, the one who lived, died, and was resurrected so we could remain a part of the intended creation, shapes our identity. Our re-creation is nurtured by and sustained in the presence of the Holy Spirit.

There are multiple ways of describing how congregations live out their calling as the people of God. The Bible has numerous metaphors or images that portray our chosen relationship with God and one another: the Body of Christ, the reign of God, the disciples of Christ, the people of God, the faithful remnant, and so on. The New Testament describes the gifts of the Spirit and the fruits of the Spirit. One thing is clear: we are united through God in Jesus Christ. Individually we bring different gifts and forms of leadership for ministry, but we form a whole. Our parent is God, our brother is Jesus, and the Holy Spirit sustains our interconnected and profound identity.

KEY ELEMENTS OF IDENTITY CONNECTIONS

Identity connections occur in a variety of ways in black congregational life. People from different genders, age groups, educational levels, and types of households commute back and forth to large, medium-sized, and small churches. Some are more open to new possibilities than others. Some come for the preaching and traditional worship, while others value the ministry with youth and children. Most have strong feelings about their church's ministry and mission and are committed to its future. (Other indicators of congregational identity, from Project 2000, can be found in Appendix B.)

MARY

Mary is a senior citizen, grandmother, and lifelong church attendee. Because of her age, she has become dependent on the church's transportation department for her travel back and forth to services. This is her story of getting there.

"If it weren't for my church, I would miss out on service every week. My children are all grown and have moved away. I am active enough to live on my own, but I have been told that it is not as safe for me to drive myself anymore. My church (which is in a major city) has a transportation committee for those of us without vehicles, and it provides rides to service. Because of where I live and its proximity to the church, I was put on the transportation list. I appreciate this because not only does this allow me to get to church, it also affords me time to interact with others while en route. Most of the people on the van with me are of the same age, so we talk a lot about service and the pastor's sermon, and we tell stories about our grandchildren. Wednesdays and Sundays are always my favorite days of the week. Sometimes I get lonely, and I look to my church as a second family. I appreciate that people take time out of their days to make mine a little easier."

Congregational Size

The media has given so much attention to the large-membership churches of our country that one might assume that the large or so-called mega church is the norm in American society. That is not the case at all. In fact the majority of faith communities across the United States are made up of approximately one hundred active adults. The small-membership church is much more the standard than is the larger congregation. For a variety of reasons, people who gather for worship on Sundays seem to do so in settings that are relatively small. In part this enables them to know the majority of other members on a deeper level than is the case in the mega church setting. Larger churches among other things provide the greater possibility of anonymity than would be possible in the smaller-membership churches. Churches that have one-hundred-plus adults plus children provide an arena where relationships can and do develop and thus enhance identity.

African American churches are similar to the rest of the congregations in this country: most are relatively small in size. In Atlanta, where we teach, one black church boasts of twenty thousand members: New Birth Missionary Church. The church and its pastor, Bishop Eddie Long, are active in the city and hence influence a variety of social, political, and economic activities in and beyond the city. A church of this size is the great exception and not the rule. Most African American faith communities that gather for worship

Congregation Size

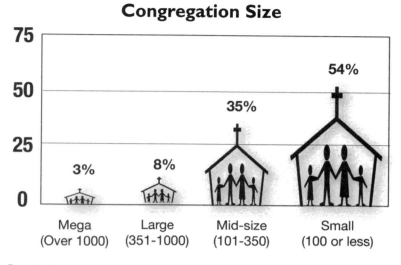

3%	8%	35%	54%
Mega (Over 1000)	Large (351-1000)	Mid-size (101-350)	Small (100 or less)

Despite the growing number and increasing popularity of mega churches, over half the total sample of black churches have fewer than one hundred regularly participating adult members, and slightly more than one-third are considered to be mid-size. Only 3 percent of African American congregations fall into the category of being mega churches, with more than one thousand church members.

on Sundays are much smaller in size and appear to be the preference for most black men and women.

Various estimates about the total number of black churches suggest that there may be approximately 70,000 individual congregations in existence. Of those, approximately 125 are mega churches. The smaller faith community is the overwhelming reality in America.

Gender Profile

Many denominational groups in this country still do not affirm the ordination of women. The majority of ordained clergy are men, and yet those individuals who are sitting in the pews or who do the ongoing and consistent work of these faith communities are women. The mission and ministry of black congregations is carried out by the women. If their financial and physical support were removed, the effectiveness of the local church would greatly diminish.

The black church in America is no exception to this pattern. In the Church of God in Christ and the vast majority of Baptist

Gender Profile

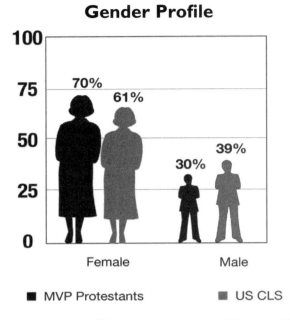

Female   Male

■ MVP Protestants   ■ US CLS

While there are fewer men (39 percent) than women (61 percent) in most US CLS congregations, women far outnumber men in even greater proportion in MVP Protestant congregations, where 70 percent of worshipers are women.

---

churches, women are not standing behind the pulpit when worship is offered. They make so many things happen in their programs and social outreach to the community, but they rarely receive the status of being the pastor. This is changing slowly in some denominational groups but still lessens the potential leadership of women who have been called to ministry by God. In our seminary setting approximately 40 percent of the students who come to us for ministerial training are women. Whether they will be able to exercise their gifts and graces across all denominational faith communities in the near future is not clear.

TINA

Tina, a twenty-seven-year-old African American woman, comes from a single-parent, female-headed household, with an up-bringing that most would consider being middle-class. Raised in the church, she confesses to know and love Jesus. Not until recently, however, did her concern for the status and role of women in the church surface. This concern about her place in the church is part of her story.

It was New Year's Eve 2004. Tina was sitting in a large urban church in Philadelphia listening to a female traveling evangelist, a regular guest at this particular church, bring the last message of the year. Like most people, Tina believed that the new year would usher in a sense of hopeful expectation, and she was excited to learn what this new year would hold for her. That night, however, would be a life-altering experience for her, if not for many other women in the congregation.

"The preacher spoke of Jezebel that night, and in her message totally destroyed the essence and power of women. She talked of the treachery and seduction of women, and how women can be very manipulative when it comes to their interactions with men." Tina was horrified: "Is this for real? Can she really be saying this to a church full of women on the eve of a new year when most of them are seeking a new and fresh beginning?" She was hurt and ashamed to be in that church that night, disgusted by the audacity of a woman in the pulpit not only collectively lumping all women into a group, but also disempowering the church as a whole.

After the events of this night, Tina was taken aback and began to reflect on her own experience in church. How many times had she been subjected to negative messages about women (usually given by men) spouted so freely from the pulpit? How often had she witnessed women sitting there, taking it, and oftentimes agreeing? She started looking at the church with a more critical eye, and began to ask questions as to why some church leaders seem to mask their own insecurities by attacking others, particularly women.

Over the last two years, Tina has not found a church to attend regularly. She has tired of the rules, practices, and constraints applied to women in the church. The surprising fact is that not only are men putting these invisible chains on the necks of

strong black women, but other women perpetrate this particular brand of sexism — an enslavement of both the mind and
the spirit.

"I come from a household of strong black women and feel
like there is worth in me that does not have to be validated by a
man, but in the church if you are a single woman you are made
to feel that something is wrong with you," says Tina.

Tina is just one among many women who profess that this is
not the God they have come to know — the God being preached
about from countless pulpits across this nation. God comes to
empower, not to tear down. "When will it stop?" they ask.

While this may not be the experience of a majority of black
women today, it does highlight some of the significant barriers women face in some congregational settings. Many Black
women experience the power of God's calling to ministry and
yet find their denominations and local churches slow to affirm
their call to pastoral ordination and leadership.

Age Profile

Another important demographic characteristic of congregational
life is the age of the members and other participants. Equal representation among all age groups would be ideal in any faith community.
To minister to all ages would be desirable, but that rarely happens
in any faith community, including black Protestant churches. In our
experience, some local churches are working with and minister to
children, young adults, the middle-aged, and seniors in effective and
vital ways, but not all congregations have that capability. Some consistently reach out to and involve young and old inside and outside
their church doors. A significant number of congregations attempt
to involve especially young people who are presently participating
at various levels as well as those who are on the margins of the
church setting. Faith communities recognize the fragile elderly and
actively work at meeting their various social, psychological, and
economic needs, but the tasks of doing so are quite challenging for
a variety of reasons — in part due to financial resources, volunteers,
and creative programs.

Our research and personal experiences with black leadership,
among both clergy and lay leadership, is that they desire to work
with at-risk children and youth. This priority is at the top of their

Age Profile

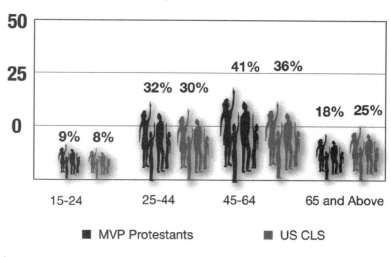

50

25

41% 36%

32% 30%

18% 25%

0

9% 8%

15-24   25-44   45-64   65 and Above

■ MVP Protestants   ■ US CLS

In most congregations across the county, those aged forty-five to sixty-four account for the largest group (36 percent), as is true in MVP congregations. The average age of worshipers in MVP congregations is forty-five, six years younger than the national average.

---

programmatic objectives but often proves to be an ongoing challenge. Many black religious leaders strive to reach out to and care for the poor and the neglected in our society. Again this is easier articulated than done. As a later chapter illustrates, the churches we have surveyed are doing an admirable job in this regard, but like all faith communities across the variety of denominational lines represented in the United States, much more is needed. African American churches are no exception to that reality. The church of Jesus Christ is making a significant difference in the lives of children and adults in our often fractured world, but the needs, at times, appear to grow with time.

Educational Background

Mainline predominantly European American churches appear to draw more highly educated adults than is the case among black congregational bodies. When compared to census data that is not altogether surprising. There continues to be a disparity in educational attainment in this country often related to racist systems that lessen

Educational Background of Worshipers

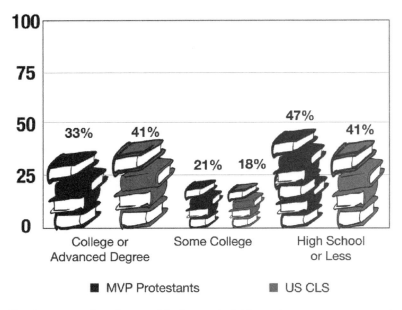

The disparity in the educational background of African Americans as compared to the national average is reflected in the educational backgrounds of worshipers. Among MVP Protestant congregations, 33 percent of worshipers are college graduates or have advanced degrees, as compared to 41 percent of CLS worshipers.

---

the opportunity for greater advancement among black people, yet the local church does have to concern itself with the results of this challenge. As one examines the trends in education over time since the civil rights era, the education levels of African American men and women have increased, but the decreasing graduation rate of black men especially in urban high schools continues to be a significant problem. Higher education often opens doors to greater opportunities, and black church leaders, according to our experience and research, appear to be conscious of that concern and have been working at creating greater support systems for young people to help reverse this trend. Nonetheless, the need for more effort and greater results remains.

Our seminary students spend time tutoring in the Atlanta public schools and continue to articulate the ever-present need for stronger

Worshipers' Family Type

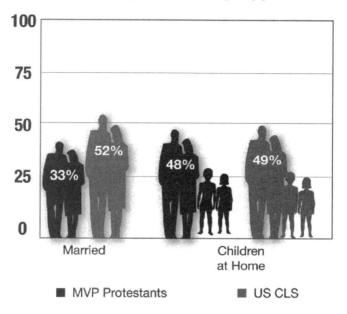

■ MVP Protestants ■ US CLS

About half of the worshipers in American congregations are married; this is not true in MVP Protestant congregations, in which only 33 percent report being married. Overall, 49 percent of worshipers have children living at home, similar to the results for MVP Protestant congregations (48 percent). The U.S. Census indicates that 52 percent of the population is currently married, and about 33 percent have children living at home.

and more comprehensive educational programs. Education is power in this country and can provide opportunities for social change and improvement in standard of living. That prison funding continues to increase while education funding remains inadequate is a fact of life that the black church has to take seriously in terms of program development as well in terms of increased advocacy at the local and national levels.

Household Type

Some people would suggest that the local church exists in part to support and strengthen families. Some politicians often debate the strengths and weaknesses of American families. They like religious leadership across the spectrum of denominational groups to affirm

the churches' apparent priority of family life. The local church, especially smaller membership faith bodies, are described as "families."
The way certain churches tend to carry out their congregational life
would in fact support that idea. Matriarchs and patriarchs in community churches often direct or significantly influence the decisions
of the local church as well as the other people who operate in this
more familial system.

Black church leaders regularly articulate this model of the church,
but as they know, the meaning of the word "family" has radically changed in our society. The so-called nuclear family is only
part of the familial picture in contemporary society. Two-parent
families among European Americans and African Americans have
changed over time. The extended family has been an important component in the black community, and its matrifocal emphasis remains
fairly consistent. When our research revealed that African American churches are made up of fewer married couples, we inferred that
this demographic reality provides additional support to the priority
of the local church to create more family-friendly programs. That
priority must continue as they develop family-like systems to help
children and adults to cope with the challenges that these statistics
suggest.

Openness to Change

A fairly commonly held belief among some social science scholars is that certain levels of societal change often occur or have
greater potential to occur when the congruence of new ideas, leaders, and supporting groups foster that potential change.[23] Some of
the results of the civil rights era illustrate a historical sample of
that belief or theory. Radical change in South Africa and well as
Brazil also give some credence to that proposition. When Dr. Martin
Luther King Jr. and many other supportive individuals articulated
the Christian message in a form that sounded somewhat new in
terms of its application to human rights and to American society
and was propagated by many black and some European American churches, significant social change occurred. Gandhi in India
and Mandela in South Africa represent other leadership aspects of
that equation along with their own respective ideas and communal
support systems.

The results of our study as well as the findings of the US CLS
program suggest that the laity and some clergy are open to the future
and are open to trying new ministry initiatives and programs. This
is good news if one is sensitive to the needs of our society and its

Worshipers' Desire for New Initiatives and Hopefulness for the Future

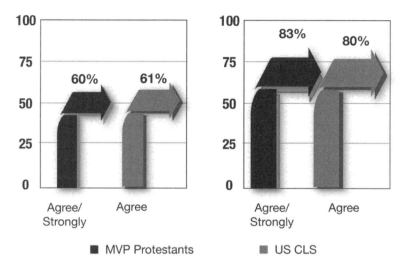

■ MVP Protestants						■ US CLS

Many worshipers in MVP congregations (60 percent) feel their congregation is always ready to try new and exciting initiatives. More than three-quarters of worshipers (83 percent) also express a sense of excitement about the future of their congregation. Likewise, many worshipers in US CLS congregations describe their congregation as willing to try new things (61 percent) and are excited about the future (80 percent).

people. With increased poverty, the absence of adequate health care insurance for too many, the problems in our elementary and high schools, substance abuse and distribution, wars and international conflicts, among other often overwhelming societal problems, new church-based approaches to issues at the very least give hope to future possibilities. If the church of Christ doubles its efforts some of these present realities may lessen over time. In the following graph, the left graphic representation reflects new initiatives, while the right one deals with excitement concerning the future.

Denominational Values

The Word of God read and preached is and should continue to be the most valued commodity in the African American church setting. Our experiences at the Interdenominational Theological Center and

Georgia State University have in no way reduced our sense of that perception. In our MVP study, that truism was found to be foremost and consistent along with our extensive exposure to black congregational life. Of course, other aspects of church life often complement that most valued asset. Bible study, the sacraments, evangelism, pastoral care, and mission all contribute to the holistic aspects of African American church involvement and importance, but preaching is at the top of the list. Those who have had marginal experience in the black religious community seem to be aware of this claim.

KIM

A thirty-five-year-old single mother working two jobs, Kim is a relatively consistently attending member of a medium-size congregation. She was asked what she valued about her church.

"As a single parent of teenage children, one of the most important things that the church provides me is a place that can minister to my kids. My local church provides programs and activities that I alone might not be able to provide for them. Allowing for them to be in fun, supervised, events with peers is something that I find invaluable.

"Another important aspect of church that I value is the support system that church provides. If I miss a Sunday or two I am almost assured of a phone call or a drop-in visitor from the church asking if things are okay, or if I need anything. This lets me know that I am part of the community, part of a larger family. It is this concern for people that I think distinguishes the church from many other community organizations.

"Lastly, the worship service itself is something I value. Many times I have had a rough day or don't feel my best. The service can leave me with a sense of strength to go on another day. Even though I may not make it as often as I should, when I am there I feel the presence of the Lord throughout the service. The preaching from the pastor gives instruction and hope to those who make up the congregation.

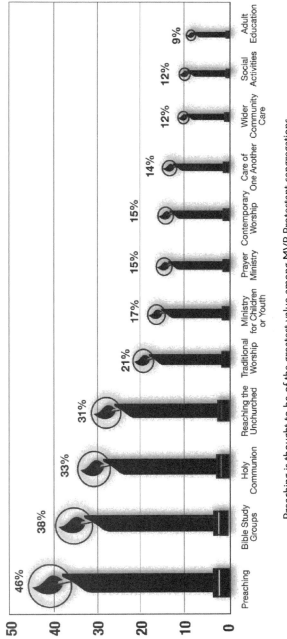

What Worshipers Value

Preaching	46%
Bible Study Groups	38%
Holy Communion	33%
Reaching the Unchurched	31%
Traditional Worship	21%
Ministry for Children or Youth	17%
Prayer Ministry	15%
Contemporary Worship	15%
Care of One Another	14%
Wider Community Care	12%
Social Activities	12%
Adult Education	9%

Preaching is thought to be of the greatest value among MVP Protestant congregations (48 percent), followed by Bible study (38 percent), Holy Communion, and reaching the "unchurched" (31 percent). On the other end of the spectrum, adult education, social activities, and wider community care are regarded of significantly lesser value to congregations.

"I value the church because it can be a source of comfort and help to people that really need it."

Committed to the Future

The future is something we religious advocates all like to talk about. The Christian gospel and the faith that has emerged as a result of Jesus and his gospel spiritually move the faithful to consider the future and work aggressively for its promises and possibilities. In the book of Revelation we are given several pictures of a God-given future. In the twenty-first chapter we are familiar with the imagery that suggests God is pulling us toward God's own future that will eventually culminate in a "new heaven and earth" (v. 1). There is the assumed perception that life will be different in God's way and in God's time. This has always been a paramount and fundamental perception of many African American Christians over the years. Our God has promised and has delivered new things and liberating realities to the social, political, and economic world in which we live. That will not change in the future. That is the future. God is calling us — individually and collectively — to respond in faith and action to God's call. A new heaven and earth are emerging. Tears will lessen and joy will increase. This basic claim of much of historical Christianity certainly is a widely held presupposition in much of black religious faith expression.

Our study reaffirmed that self-understanding. The identity of Christian churches is, in certain ways, grounded in this promise and presumed future. Our research project found most laity and pastors to be committed to the future ministry and mission; they voiced a clear vision and their implied commitment to that vision. This is quite promising. As indicated above, the results of our project and this book that has come as result of it rest on the hope that those who have given voice to their openness to change and commitment to God's future will continue into that future with greater effort and lasting results for God's people and God's planet.

This chapter has introduced the important component of con-gregational life we have called identity. Most worshipers in MVP congregations (68 percent) believe that their churches articulate a clear vision, goals, or direction for the future. The identity of a local church body originates and is sustained by many aspects of religious life. Identity has to do with people, history, and worldview. It includes character, heritage, and rituals, among others. Understanding your congregation's identity can help unleash its spiritual power.

Does Your Church Have Goals?

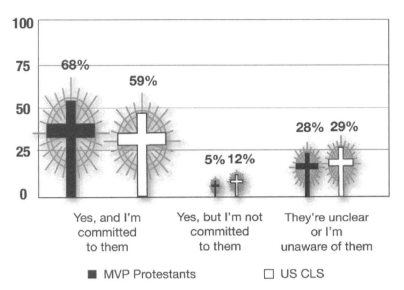

Yes, and I'm committed to them   Yes, but I'm not committed to them   They're unclear or I'm unaware of them

■ MVP Protestants   □ US CLS

Most worshipers in MVP congregations (68 percent) believe that their churches articulate a clear vision, goals, or direction for the future. However, some are not sure that the vision is clear, or that it exists (28 percent). The national average indicates that more than half of US CLS worshipers (59 percent) believe their congregations have a clear vision, while 29 percent remain unclear or unaware of what that vision is.

GROUP EXERCISES

The following exercises are brief assessment exercises (one to two hours) that Sunday school class or fellowship group can use to begin an examination of identity connection within your congregation.

Exercise I: Considering the Church's Identity

This exercise will help your congregation's members explore various components of your congregation's identity. The questions can be used individually or in any order for discussion.

- ✦ What is the history of our congregation?
- ✦ What unique events make up our history?

◆ What is our denominational tradition and local tradition?

◆ In what ways do our people see the world and its concerns?

◆ What are the important symbols of our setting?

◆ Have some symbols faded and others taken their place?

◆ What rituals, large and small, do we follow and hold as important?

◆ What is the social, political, economic, and ethnic makeup of our members and community residents?

◆ What are the characteristics of our people?

Exercise 2: Working through the Details of Your Church's Identity

Allow one to two hours for this exercise, at minimum. You may choose to work on one or two areas of identity in greater detail:

History. Make a timeline to understand how the congregation is situated within local, denominational, national, and global history.

Heritage. Examine the local and larger traditions of the church. Study both denominational and local documents that reveal aspects of its heritage. Understanding theological as well as social perspectives can be helpful.

Worldview. Use of language and ideas by members with varying political viewpoints can reveal certain aspects of the perspective of your congregation.

Symbols. Certain objects, places and events have symbolic meaning for congregants. Take note of what they mean for various members.

Rituals. List the church's formal and informal rituals and their meanings.

Demographics. Conduct walking and/or driving expeditions. Look for places people live, work, shop, play, and worship. Observe how people get from place to place. Look for things that are new or easy to miss (new businesses, homes, places where homeless people live, etc.). Identify the local religious environment (how many churches are in your neighborhood?). Identity traffic patterns, improved or deteriorating property, and so forth. Keep notes on what you observe.

Character. Identify where congregation members live, work, shop and play.

IDENTITY CONNECTIONS
REFLECTION QUESTIONS

1. What important beliefs, religious practices, and rituals does your congregation identify as distinctive to its denominational heritage and identity?

2. How can you plan for an identity assessment of your congregation?

3. Why do you think your congregation cares about the ministries in which it is involved?

4. How are children and youth cared for in your congregation?

5. Can you identify ways to meet needs for elders in the congregation and beyond?

6. Elaborate on the relationship between how well members of your congregation understand the church's mission (purpose) and their level of participation.

7. In what ways can your congregation imagine, plan, and develop strategies to assess its spiritual vitality?

Chapter Three

Power Connections
inside the Congregation

Our knowledge of God is in and through each other. Our knowledge of each other is in and through God. We act together and find our good in each other and in God, and our power grows together, or we deny our relation and reproduce a violent world where no one experiences holy power.
— Beverly Wildung Harrison, *Making Connections*[24]

Spiritual connectedness and congregational identity are key components of congregational life. What happens inside the walls of black churches is also of vital importance. More than women and men gathering for worship, study, and service, lifetime relationships are often built and sustained. There is power in being together in one setting and experiencing the totality of life's joys and pains.

African American life in the United States has always been grounded in the need for and perseverance of congregational life within the church. Being there and participating in church activities that are provided on a regular basis are critical to the power of blacks as a people — a people who have known tremendous pressure in a society that often perpetuates disunity and disconnectedness. Church gatherings provide black individuals, families, and extended families with opportunities to be together in safe and self-determined ways in a world that has overwhelmingly discounted them and their institutions. The presence of the Holy Spirit is assumed when black church folk come together in a specific and special congregational setting. Being inside together is absolutely necessary for the sustenance of spiritual power connections, but also for the activities that are advanced beyond the walls of the faith community. Inside power is a nonnegotiable reality of African American religiosity.

Worshipers connect with others in congregations through group activities (such as church school, prayer and study groups, and fellowships or clubs), serving in leadership roles, and collective financial support. This chapter explores worshipers' activities within the faith community and examines how these connections relate to one another. It will look at ways that worshipers are involved in their congregations, leadership roles that members hold within their congregations, ways that worshipers feel they belong to their congregations, the role that friendship plays within congregations, the connections between leaders and worshipers, and the role of financial support in connecting people to a congregation and its mission. Additionally, this chapter presents a framework to conduct an assessment of your congregation regarding its inside connections.

BIBLICAL FOUNDATION

When the day of Pentecost had come, all were together in one place. And suddenly from heaven there came a sound like the rush of a violent wind, and it filled the entire house where they were sitting.... All of them were filled with the Holy Spirit and began to speak in other languages, as the Spirit gave them the ability. — Acts 2:1–2, 4 NRSV

We remember that your church was born in wind and fire,
Not to sweep us heavenward
Like a presumptuous tower, but to guide us down
The dusty roads of this world
So that we may lift up the downcast,
Heal the broken,
Reconcile what is lost,
And bring peace amidst unrest.
— Garth House, *Litanies for All Occasions*[25]

The Acts of the Apostles is the first history of a Christian congregation. It tells the story of Jesus' life and sets the stage for reflection by the members of this new Christian movement. The story throughout Acts reflects on the movement's own identity and the meaning of its beginnings. It tells the story of how the first congregation became aware of who they were, how they analyzed the power of the Holy Spirit in their midst, and how they were then moved to action, all the while reflecting on the role of God in their lives, calling them to action with a purpose. These four processes — awareness, analysis, action, and reflection — are a continual cycle in which healthy congregations are engaged. Certainly, a congregation goes through this cycle during its formative stages, and it goes through this cycle over and over as it grows and tries to live out God's call on the congregation and its members.

Early Christian communities presented a model of the appropriate interaction with the larger world and of their life within their community. They depicted the ideal of Greek friendship — friends are "of one heart and one soul" and "have all things in common" — and the Deuteronomistic picture of Israel's sacred beginnings in the wilderness, when "there was no needy person among them" (Acts 4:32–37 NRSV). The early Christian congregations had power in being together in one setting and experiencing the totality of life's joys and pains together. There is also another way of telling the story of the early Christian congregations, a way that still has broader meaning for Christian congregations today. It begins and ends in heaven. It is the story of Jesus, who is a divine figure and who came into the world, returned to heaven, and sent his Spirit to be with each of us. The Spirit was key for helping a beleaguered community of Christians to interpret the meaning of their experience. It was the Spirit that gave power to these early congregations to develop a communal self-identity.

The Christian message was brought to the cities of the Roman Empire by ordinary people who moved about preaching and establishing Christian communities. According to the account in Acts, when an apostle arrived in a new city, he made his first contact at the synagogue (as at Thessalonica, Acts 17:1–2), or in the Jewish residential quarter, or among the craftsmen whose trade he knew (as with Priscilla and Aquila at Corinth, Acts 18:2–4). The apostle would often lodge with these initial converts and make further contacts among a circle of acquaintances at home or at work. For the most part, however, converts first heard the Christian message on a more intimate scale of personal contact, through friends and acquaintances who then took them to one of the group's weekly meetings.

This pattern of intimacy with fellow Christians is still foundational for Christian congregations today, no matter how small or large the congregation is. At its core, all Christian congregations have inside connections that are unique to that congregation. For the remainder of this chapter, we look at components of some of the ways these inside connections are important to the way a congregation lives out God's call in its life.

SHAWNDRA

Only on reflection did Shawndra really understand what it meant to experience a true sense of belonging. She didn't really understand it until she moved away and realized what she'd had growing up. Having been a member of her church for almost twenty years—nearly 80 percent of her life—she believed she felt a sense of belonging within her church; although looking back, perhaps she had just taken it for granted. Between going to Sunday services most of the time, Sunday school, Bible study, choir rehearsals, dinners, and so many other church functions, she realized that the time she spent with her church family rivaled the time she spent with most members of her own family. So it was not surprising that she felt such a severe sense of loss when she moved to another state and was, for the first time in twenty years, away from her church.

Shawndra's sense of belonging within her church was more than just a feeling. When she walked into her church, through the front doors, into the sanctuary, and down the aisle to a pew, she had felt a sense of ownership. "This was my home; it was a sanctuary to me in so many senses of the word, "she exclaimed. "Maybe it's because I've 'let it go' in this place. I've become emotional; shed tears openly, sobbed until I couldn't stand, and comforted others who did the same.

"When I really think about it, I've experienced so many different relationships there as well. I have felt loved, comforted, hurt, betrayed, supported, and let down. I've watched children be born and grow up... watched those who seemed so young at one point grow old, many even passing on. More than anything, however, I have, in so many ways, let my church raise me. My church family reaffirmed the values I was being taught at home, but they also took a sense of responsibility for me as I grew up. I remember times I heard my grandmother reassure some of the women I would sit with while she sang in the choir that they could "get me if I acted up." This was also the place where the seeds of my spiritual life were first planted."

During the eleventh year of her membership at the church, while a student at a local college, Shawndra learned that her pastor would be retiring. Utterly shocked, she feared her congregation would be lost. It was like losing the patriarch of a large family, with no successor in place. Shawndra's church remained without a pastor for three years and nine months, during which time her congregation ran the gamut of change. Upon reflection, however, Shawndra was mostly reminded of how the church stuck together, prayed together and supported each other. "I remember the sense of betrayal I felt as some of the members left, but my sense of belonging, faithfulness, and loyalty were what made me stay," Shawndra says. "When I first moved away, I remember sitting in the church I had been visiting and for a moment I thought that maybe I was being led to finally join. I wasn't ready to move on, though, to call myself a member of another church. Although I enjoyed the services I was lonely for the sense of comfort I had only experienced at one other church. I guess the point is that belonging for me was inevitable. It was the product of a complete familial experience. Although we did not share the same blood, we were connected and bound by the blood of Jesus, and that made us family."

KEY ELEMENTS
OF INSIDE CONNECTIONS

Worshipers connect with others in their congregation through group activities, leadership roles, and financial support. Inside connections consist of all the activities involving worshipers and congregational leadership.

Today, more people of faith are seeking churches according to the style of worship and music rather than differences in denominational doctrine or geographical location.[26] Utilizing the rubric of awareness, analysis, action, and reflection, this chapter examines the ways congregations involve worshipers and leaders, the ways in which people feel they belong to their congregations, the ways people make friends within their congregations, and the ways that financial support contributes to being a part of the congregational team.

Involving Worshipers

According to our research, more than 75 percent of worshipers in black congregations are active in small group activities within their churches. About half are active within group activities such as Sunday school or church school. Forty-six percent are involved in prayer, discussion, or Bible study groups, and 44 percent are connected to fellowships, clubs, and other social groups. Black congregations have a higher than national average of ministry activities that also includes a higher than average number of people within the congregation participating in the ministries. This is a very significant fact about black congregations. They are widely active in a broad range of ministries and activities that help and support the communities within which they are located. This is primarily due to the historical role the black church has played within its community. As the spiritual, historical, cultural, and civic nexus of African American life, the black church is viewed as the single most important social institution in the black community.

This figure reflects the high levels of worshiper participation in small group activities within congregations. Because of the social context in which the black church existed during the eighteenth, nineteenth, and twentieth centuries in America, participation in small-group church schools, prayer and discussion groups, and social fellowship groups were often the only socially acceptable activities available for African Americans. These groups supported fundamental commitments to social as well as theological freedom.

Historically, the black church knew from the beginning that its paramount mission was freedom. Because the black Protestant church was born in a time and place of human bondage, the church's emphasis on freedom was generally assumed to focus on issues related to slavery. This assumption, however, is incorrect and limiting. The freedom the black church has sought is the freedom to belong to God, to worship God and to participate in the divine agenda without hindrance from other human beings.

In the early black church, the first emphasis was on getting to know God and coming to terms with the fact that black people were not "cursed of God." A second concern was to destroy the slave system by refusing to cooperate with it. When the slave era finally ended after the Civil War, the black church sponsored schools,

Participation in Small Group Activities

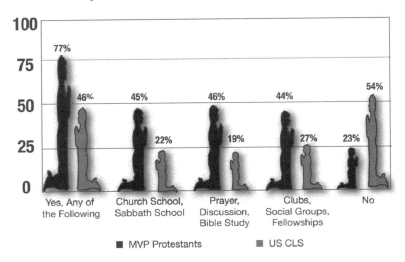

Overall, 77 percent of MVP worshipers participate in small group activities within their churches. Almost half are active in group activities such as Sunday school, church school, or Sabbath school (45 percent); prayer, discussion, or Bible study groups (46 percent); or fellowships, clubs, or other social groups (44 percent) — in stark contrast to the US CLS report of only 46 percent of worshipers engaging in some small-group church activity.

saving societies, insurance companies, banks, and a variety of social services. This struggle for full freedom continues even into the twenty-first century. The traditional practices and communal responsibilities of the black church continue to address the challenges of today and tomorrow. Black churches are characterized by their communal quest for human freedom and justice.

Involving Leaders

Of the laity surveyed in the MVP study, 74 percent reported that they hold at least one leadership position in their congregation (such as governing board, committee, choir or usher, church school teacher, etc.) — nearly double the average reported by US CLS congregations. Why are African American congregations so leadership heavy? How is leadership perceived in African American congregations? How does ministerial leadership contribute to the support or constraint of lay leadership? What is the role of gender in

Congregants Holding Leadership Roles

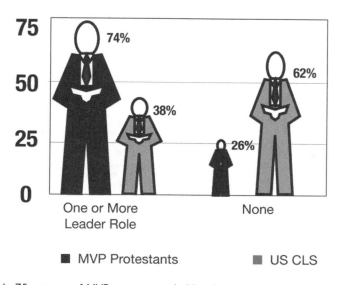

■ MVP Protestants   **■ US CLS**

Nearly 75 percent of MVP congregants hold at least one leadership position in their congregation (such as member of a governing board or committee, choir member, usher, church school teacher, etc.) — far exceeding the 38 percent of worshipers in the US CLS study who serve as church leaders.

the perception of leadership roles within the congregation? MVP researchers used these inquiry questions to examine leadership, discourse, symbols, and mentoring in producing lay leaders and shaping the beliefs and values of congregations. Of particular interest was examining the role of women in church leadership, internal systems of support for women to exercise leadership, and spiritual gifts as part of women's spiritual development. In addition to the primary MVP survey instrument utilized by parishioners, church pastors and church administrators were also surveyed in separate questionnaires. Data derived from the leader and administrator surveys provided evidence regarding the current roles of women in leadership positions of the church.

The African American church is known and highly regarded as a focal point for social involvement within the African American community. Although black churches throughout history have been

Strong Approval of Women Pastors, by Level of Pastor Respondents' Education

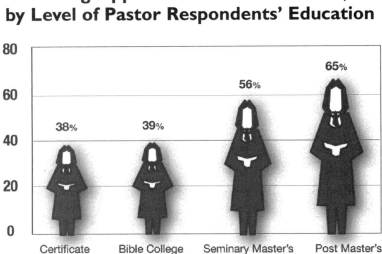

The presence of women in the pulpit has traditionally been an issue of great controversy among African American denominations and churches. In the total sample of black clergy, the better educated the pastors, the more favorable they are toward women pastors.

involved in seeking political equality and justice for African Americans, the inequality of black women in terms of class and gender remains an unresolved issue. Even though the principal programs of the black church rely disproportionately on women for their support and success, all of the traditional black religious denominations tend to have congregations made up mostly of women and are led primarily by men. Some denominations that typically have middle-class congregations, most notably the black Methodists, have displayed less gender bias when compared to Holiness denominations, which, in turn, appear to demonstrate less class bias and tend to attract poorer, less educated African Americans.

The ordination of women has been a controversial issue in the history of the black Protestant church, and women as ordained clergy have been historically underrepresented in the black church. For the most part, men have monopolized the ordained ministry. Many of the founders of black churches ignored the unfairness of some of their practices, even though these practices were analogous to the injustices of the white society against African Americans.[27]

In recent years, many traditional denominations have ordained a greater number of women ministers, but organizational hurdles have placed a stained-glass ceiling on women's opportunities to attain either pastorates in larger congregations or higher-ranking ecclesiastical posts. Black women have had limited leadership roles available to them. Since church leadership has been the primary mechanism for entrance into the political arena — as evidenced by many prominent black political leaders who are also clergy, such as Andrew Young, Adam Clayton Powell Jr. and Jesse Jackson — women have therefore been limited in political leadership opportunities as well.

Even with the prestige of black women at national church conventions, and in spite of the growth of black women's public speaking capabilities, the distinction between speaking and teaching as female roles and preaching as a male role is maintained as the norm in many black churches. It has been suggested that this gender division of labor was an accommodation to the dominant culture's reading of biblical texts on women's roles.[28] On all organizational levels, women are concentrated in areas of church work traditionally done by women rather than in top leadership positions. Women are accorded greater participation on the decision-making boards of smaller churches, but not the larger ones. Women are found in the membership and on the staffs of church-based agencies that are connected to missions and education, the historic channels for women's work, but seldom in the organizations that could serve as springboards to political activity.[29] Black women have been rewarded for their accomplishments in backbone or supportive roles primarily through leadership roles of church-based ministries as well as administrative roles within the church.

Social welfare was not considered a primary role for men in African American culture; therefore, this activity was delegated to the women of the church.[30] Women founded ministries that catered to urban areas. In these ministries, they preached, ran day care and food distribution centers, and educated those who sought them out. Fund raising was only one of the ways women demonstrated that they, in essence, were the foundation of the church even though men were at the forefront and received most of the recognition. Money was the means to attain success for African missions, and women were the principal players in raising it. Because opportunities for women within the traditional ministry of black churches were limited, the missionary profession was appealing to many African American women, giving them the opportunity to pursue leadership roles not normally available to them in America. In other words, black women are deeply involved as leaders *in* congregations but much less so as leaders *of* congregations. For both men and women, being involved at the leadership level in the congregation helped them feel connected inside their congregation.

Belonging

The vast majority of worshipers within most black American congregations report a strong sense of belonging to their congregations and even claim that this sense of belonging has been growing, although about 24 percent of the respondents in the MVP study reported it was steady or declining. Overall, black congregations across all denominations have shown slower declines in membership than do mainline white congregations. This lower rate of change among denominations of the black church may be understood to be primarily a result of strong pastoral leadership within black congregations and the strong sense of communal power within black religious institutions generally.

Making Friends

Are worshipers developing friendships with others in their congregations? About 73 percent of MVP Protestant worshipers say some or all of their close friends are members of the same congregation. The significance of friendships is essential to the embodiment of communal power found within black congregations, for it was only within the church that the experience of self-governance provided blacks with the opportunity to practice basic rights of citizenship long before the basic rights became constitutionally guaranteed and politically enacted for them.[31]

For women, the black church has traditionally provided a strong base for building, developing, and sustaining friendships. Women's conventions within their denominations are among the largest organized groups of black women in the United States.[32] Women serve in myriad roles in black churches as evangelists, missionaries, stewardesses, deaconesses, lay readers, writers on religious subjects, Sunday school teachers, musicians, choir members and directors, ushers, nurses, custodians, caterers and hostesses for church dinners, secretaries and clerks, counselors, recreation leaders, and directors of vacation Bible schools. Women are also designated "mothers of the church," an honorific title usually reserved for the wife of the founder/pastor. All of the seven mainline black denominations are characterized by a predominantly female membership

Sense of Belonging among Worshipers

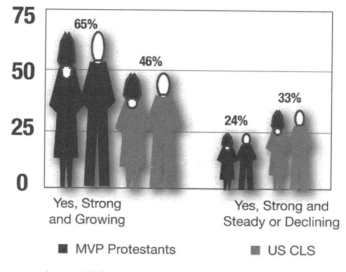

Most respondents in MVP congregations reported a strong sense of belonging in their congregations, similar to that found in typical congregations nationwide. The vast majority (65 percent) also claimed that this sense of belonging is on the rise, while only 24 percent reported that it remains steady or is declining.

and a largely male leadership, despite the fact that the major programs of the black church in politics, economics, and music depend heavily upon women for their promotion and success.[33] Women especially have strong friendships and are deeply connected to one another in black congregations, which greatly contributes to black spiritual power.

Giving

Black churches have historically operated with a strong sense of self-determination and faith. This self-determination and deep faith developed from the horrific experience of slavery. From the days when early black congregations were underground institutions, the congregations served as a place of refuge where destitute African Americans could find clothing, food, housing, and spiritual sustenance. Over the last several decades, however, resources available to many churches from individual donors, government, and the private sector have seriously dwindled. A confluence of factors seems to

Friends at Church

100

75

50   73%   67%

25

0

Yes, Some or All of My
Close Friends Attend Here

■ MVP Protestants   ■ US CLS

Congregational life can contribute to the formation of meaningful relationships
with others. About 73 percent of MVP Protestant worshipers say most of their
close friends are members of the same congregation. This is somewhat reflective
of the national congregational profile in which 67 percent of US CLS worshipers
also say they have close friends in their congregations.

be responsible for this situation: upper- and middle-income African
Americans relocating from urban to suburban areas; the change
from an industrial society to a technology- and information-based
society, which has eliminated jobs once held by African Americans,
who are now unemployed; and the neutral-to-negative attitudes of
many younger African Americans toward the church.[34]

The degree to which the black church has been able to financially maintain and expand its community programs is unclear. In
the ITC Project 2000 study, a majority of the full sample of black
churches surveyed reported they were financially stable, and only
a small percentage of congregations reported they were in serious
financial difficulty.[35] In the MVP study, we found that 98 percent

Giving as a Percentage of Income

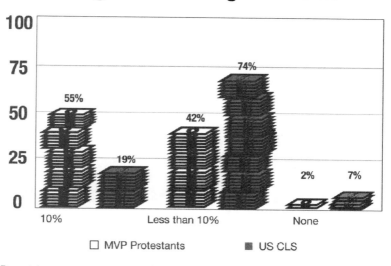

Financial support connects people to a congregation and its mission. in MVP Protestant congregations, 98 percent of worshipers make financial contributions — including the 55 percent of worshipers who regularly tithe (contribute 10 percent or more of their net income to their church). Nationally, 93 percent of worshipers make financial contributions to their churches, and only 19 percent tithe.

of Protestant congregational members make financial contributions, including 55 percent who regularly give 10 percent or more of their net income to their congregations.[36] In a survey study, Dr. Emmett Carson, president of the Minnesota Foundation, found that over two-thirds (68 percent) of all charitable dollars in the African American community go to a church. About half (52 percent) of the African Americans surveyed reported having contributed food, clothing, or other property to a charitable organization, and 50 percent volunteered to work with some type of charitable organization.[37] These findings present a complex perspective about the financial health of African American churches in America. Most African Americans view their church positively and often do not have complete knowledge regarding the financial situation of the church.

The mega church phenomenon of the last twenty years requires its own analysis, because much of what occurs in a mega church cannot apply to the understanding of what occurs in the majority

Financial Health of Black Churches

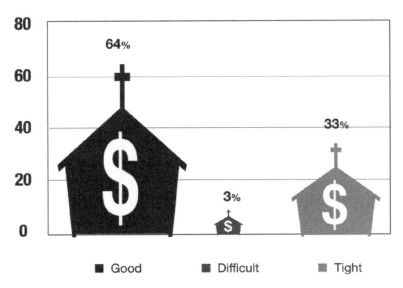

■ Good   ■ Difficult   ■ Tight

Despite the great disparity in African American household income as compared to the national average, a sizeable majority of black churches are financially stable (64 percent). The financial picture is even brighter among black Baptist churches (73 percent). Only a small percentage of black congregations (3 percent) are facing serious financial difficulty.

of churches in America. A mega church receives the designation of "mega"[38] if it has a regular weekly worship attendance of over 2,000. Mega churches represent a very small percentage (less than 1 percent) of the total number of congregations of any denomination. Of this less than 1 percent, black mega churches constitute only a very small number, approximately 6 percent, of the total number of mega churches. Mega churches are predominantly a phenomenon of the suburbs of very large cities. Sixty-three percent are located in or around cities of 250,000 or more, with 23 percent in cities with a population between 50,000 and 250,000. Nearly three-quarters of the churches are located in the older parts or newer suburbs of these large cities. Most of the congregations have some minority racial presence. Nearly 50 percent of the white congregations have 10 percent or more regular minority adult participants. Twelve

Correlation of Church Size and Growth and Financial Health

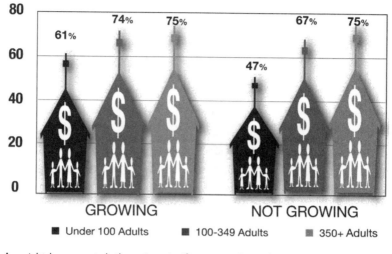

As might be expected, there is a significant correlation between church size and financial health. Larger churches of the Baptist denomination are more likely to report being in good financial health than smaller churches of any denomination. Similarly, churches that have grown 5 percent or more since 1995 are more likely to demonstrate good financial health. However, even among growing churches, larger churches still have a distinct financial advantage.

percent of churches without a black majority have a significant (10–49 percent) black presence among their regular attendees.[39] The financial health of a church depends on its size and financial resources. Generally speaking, black church members with higher household incomes gave more to the church, but lower-income members appeared more committed to tithing than higher-income members.[40] Churches with a large proportion of adult members with family incomes of less than twenty thousand dollars a year are significantly less likely to be financially stable than churches with adults with higher incomes. The churches in the best financial health are clearly the larger churches, with relatively few low-income families. Urbanicity also has an effect on giving in black churches. Members living in urban areas gave more than those in suburban or rural areas. Those residing in rural areas gave the lowest amounts to the church, owing to the relative economic advantages and needs of urban and suburban areas.[41]

BETH

The idea of giving is a biblical concept, outlined in Malachi 3:10: "Bring all the tithes into the storehouse." In many congregations giving is said to be a form of worship or praise. There are times when giving can become a burden or frustration to the people in a church. This is Beth's story about that kind of experience. Beth is an upper-middle-class single woman who has a good job and makes good money, but she recalls a time when she felt the church went too far in asking for money from people:

"I was visiting a friend's church for the first time; although I am not new to church, this was my first time in this particular congregation. After a wonderful service, where the spirit was so high, the preacher blew the roof off of the house, I felt so good in my spirit that I was excited when the time of giving had arrived. Immediately I went to my purse to write my check, but the pastor got the mike and started a fifty-dollar line. This was more than I had anticipated giving that day, but God had blessed me so during the service that I wrote the check and stood up. I only can assume that the pastor was not happy with the number of people that were in line so he instructed the deacons to count the offering at the table. After that count the pastor called for a forty-dollar line. This incremental giving continued on for forty-five minutes until finally the pastor said anyone giving under ten dollars get into the line. My spirit was crushed. I had lost all of the joy that I once was feeling. Not only that, but half of the congregation had exited the church. Being a visitor, that experience left such a negative impression about that church that I told myself and my friend that I could not attend any more services there again. Giving should be a joyous experience; it should not be looked at as theft. It seemed as if the pastor was trying to hold the people by their collective ankles and shake the change out of their pockets. This is not what the Bible asks of us as givers. It does not demand our last, but it requires a tenth of our firstfruits. God is not a stickup person that demands all you have. The blessing is not in the amount you give, but in the obedience and mind-set in which you give.

"I would pray that this is not a practice that is widespread in churches, but part of me believes that many churches do perpetuate this type of mentality. I have not let this one experience stop me from giving to the church in the future, but I have become wary of the preacher for whom money seems to be the main motivation for a sign of commitment. God loves a cheerful giver, and the church should always remember that."

When giving flows from spiritual vitality and deep relationships within a faith community, contributing financially to that church's ministry and mission seems more natural. This was not Beth's experience.

Being a Team

Do worshipers feel there is a strong connection between leaders and worshipers in their congregation? Most worshipers in the United States agree that there is a good match between their congregation and the minister or pastor, yet one of the biggest complaints within congregations — no matter the size, denomination, or pastoral leadership — is that 20 percent of the people in the congregation are doing 80 percent of the work. Often, one problem is not having adequate volunteers. Another problem relates to involving volunteers in inefficient and ineffective planning and executing of ministry, and it all begins with poorly organized meetings.

Those Church Meetings!

Building sound church leadership typically results from practicing some accepted team-building principles. Leadership teams often go through several major phases, including the following:

Forming. When members are beginning to assemble, individually they consider "What am I here for?" "Who else is here?" "Who am I comfortable with?" and so on. During this stage, it's important to get members involved and for them to develop a personal involvement and commitment to their task. During this initial phase, which

Presence of Teamwork in Church

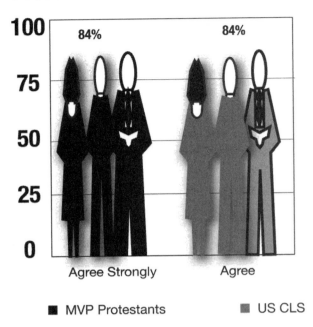

Most worshipers (84 percent) in MVP Protestant congregations and in the US CLS study either agree or strongly agree that a spirit of teamwork exists between the pulpit and the pews—that there is a good match between their congregations and their ministers, pastors, or priests that works toward the common good of the church.

includes members introducing themselves to each other, you want members to develop a commitment to the project or ministry.

Storming. During this stage, members are beginning to voice their individual differences, trying to join with others who share the same beliefs, and trying to jockey for position in the group. Therefore, it's important for members to continue to be highly involved, including voicing their concerns in order to feel represented and understood. The team leader should focus on gaining clarity of views, achieving consensus and recording decisions.

Norming. In this stage, members begin to share their common commitment to the purpose of the church ministry/activity, including its overall goals and how it will reach these goals.

Performing. In this stage, the team is humming. Members are actively participating in the team process in order to achieve the goals of the group or the congregation. During this stage, the style of leadership becomes more indirect as members take on stronger participation and involvement in the group process.

Closing and Celebration. At this stage, it's clear to everyone that the team has achieved its overall purpose. Acknowledging accomplishment is critical lest members feel unfulfilled and skeptical about future team efforts.

For a further discussion of basic principles for church leadership, see Appendix C.

TAKING A DEEPER LOOK AT YOUR INSIDE CONNECTIONS: CONGREGATIONAL ASSESSMENT

Congregational assessment is a disciplined study of the congregation. There is a connection between bringing men and women into a personal relationship with Jesus Christ and responsible church membership. The care of members within the community of the congregation — how persons are accepted and find mutual support — is reflected in the way a congregation lives out its mission and ministry. Each congregation is guided by the theological tenets that guide its mission and ministry. Each of the tenets undergirding particular congregations determines how we act. Congregations need spiritual and social contact to develop properly.

Congregational assessment is a process that starts by determining where your congregation is now and examines theological, social, cultural, philosophical, educational, and other connections within your congregation. A congregational assessment utilizes your congregational strengths to determine its future.

The basic assumption of congregational assessment is that your congregation is ready for such a process. Understanding your congregational culture is essential for communication with the people in your congregation and the people with whom your congregation wants and needs to interact. Congregations have multiple layers of connections: spiritual, social, economic, community, and denominational. These layers of connections are to be found within the congregation as well as outside. Identifying your congregational strengths will help your congregation understand the call God has placed on your community to do God's work in the world.

There are practical pressures facing many churches today: political, societal, educational, and economic, to name a few. What
happens in congregations is theological. People of faith are looking
for ways to make sense of their lives and to devise ways of relating
to the divine powers within and beyond them. More importantly,
people who lead congregations need to think seriously about their
environments.

An effective congregational assessment includes and gathers information from the congregation's severest critics as well as from its
most enthusiastic promoters. It is important for less vocal members
to have a voice in the congregational assessment process. Throughout the process, you will be looking for patterns between seemingly
unrelated issues. Information may be revealed that a congregation
does not want to see. For example, an analysis of leadership and
decision-making styles may reveal patterns that members may want
to change. Congregational assessment opens the way to congregational self-understanding and corporate participation. The study
should be regulated by an established order of inquiry, a discipline
for gathering information, and a set of rules for organizing and interpreting information. The assessment will then be available to any
interested member who can and will review the process, conclusion,
and judgments. Be aware, though, that the dynamics of congregational assessment may have intended and unintended consequences
related to the process of assessment. These issues may be related to
privacy, the type of questions people will ask, and how they will
ask them. Some challenges may arise in going through the process
of systematically observing your congregation.

A congregation may conduct a self-assessment when it is at a
turning point in its history. A congregation may also find a self-
assessment useful when it needs to make decisions about particular
aspects of the congregation itself:

Strategic decisions. Should the congregation grow? Merge?
Shrink? Change its mission?

Program decisions. Should programs be expanded? Should two
or several programs be integrated? Should new ministries be offered?

Staffing decisions. Should staff with different skills be hired to
support the mission? Should the congregation let some staff go? If
so, who?

Other reasons for undertaking a congregational assessment
might be less specific; for example, the self-assessment might have
the following objectives:

+ To identify the congregation's strengths and weaknesses — a first step toward improvement

+ To identify issues and problems before correction becomes difficult or impossible

+ To identify the needs that should be addressed through specific action

+ To identify human and other resources the congregation can use to effectively improve its performance

+ To document the desired outcomes of the congregation's activities

+ To generate information useful in planning and decision-making

+ To provide members and other stakeholders (denominational leaders, etc.) with information about the congregation's performance

Clarify your reasons for undertaking the self-assessment. Once you are clear about this, you will find it easier to determine the scope of the assessment, the depth of data you will require, and the focus in terms of issues (such as identifying the type of ministry involvement in which your congregation wants and needs to be involved, its capacity for ministry, its motivation for particular ministries, the environment to initiate and/or maintain ministries, etc.). Exercise 1 at the end of this chapter will help your congregation identify its reasons for conducting a congregational assessment. For an in-depth discussion related to preparing for a congregational assessment, see Appendix D: Preparing for a Congregational Self-Assessment.

GROUP EXERCISES

The following exercises are brief assessment exercises (one to two hours) that Sunday school or fellowship groups can utilize to begin an examination of inside connections within your congregation.

Exercise 1: Doing a Culture Audit of the Congregation

(Note: We recommend that you read Appendix D before undertaking this exercise.)

Purpose

Even though the specifics of individual congregational cultures vary widely, all congregations have four cultural components: symbols, language, values, and norms. These components contribute to harmony and strife in the congregation as well as harmony and strife with society in general.

Many congregations that are experiencing rapid changes find that before they begin a self-assessment, they want or need to go through the process of examining very basic cultural components of their congregation. This level of analysis often facilitates the process of self-assessment, especially if your congregation is experiencing changes in its membership due to age of your members (increase/decease of particular age groups) or a change in cultural groups that participate in your congregation.

The purpose of the culture audit is to provide the congregation with a list of areas within which data can be gathered respecting congregational motivation for ministry development or other aspects of change in which the congregation may want to engage. Some of the questions are designed to take the pulse of the congregation and could be used in animating focus groups of staff members or people in leadership roles.

Instructions

Individually answer as many of the questions below as you can. Then, in a group, discuss your answers and whether one can answer all the questions. Are most people agreed on their answers?

1. What kinds of people are involved in this congregation? Who are the real leaders? Who gets ahead? (These questions provide information on the informal reward and power systems, as well as identifying any heroes.)

2. What is it like to be part of this congregation? (This question provides a real overview of the congregation's culture.)

3. Why is the congregation successful? (This helps describe what areas are perceived as important.)

4. Can you clearly define the congregation's values or beliefs and norms of acceptable behavior?

5. What is the congregation's culture now? How strongly and uniformly does this culture exist across the congregation?

6. Are people considered important to this congregation?

7. What skills and actions are rewarded?

8. What is the history of the congregation?

9. Does the congregation focus inwardly, rather than to the outside world; that is, does it have only a short-term focus?

10. How frequent is the turnover of personnel?

11. What are the "war stories" and anecdotes of this congregation?

12. What are the major events in this congregation's past?

13. How are people new to the congregation assimilated?

14. What matters have a high priority in this congregation? What matters have a low priority?

15. Overall, how would you describe the culture of your congregation?

Exercise 2: Getting Ready for Congregational Assessment

Ask a group of lay leaders in your congregation to reflect individually on these questions, then use the list as a tool to collectively discuss the congregation's readiness for congregational assessment.

1. Is the congregation facing the need to make strategic decisions? Would a self-assessment help in the decision making?

2. To what extent do the senior lay leaders in your congregation support the change process? Does the staff have confidence in the lay leaders' ability to engage in change management?

3. To what extent is any individual (pastor or lay leader) willing to champion the process and capable of doing so?

4. Does the congregation have a clear vision of where it wishes to go?

5. Are major changes already going on within the congregation that might slow down the process or interfere with it?

6. Does the congregation have access to resources to carry out the process?

7. Do people inside the congregation have adequate skills to undertake this process?

8. When was the last major congregational change? To what extent was it successful? Did it energize the membership or lower their morale?

9. To what extent are the leaders and staff comfortable with the use of congregational data? To what extent does congregational data exist?

10. Is this a good time for change? Would another time be better? Are there future incentives for change to occur now?

11. What are the positive, negative, neutral, or cultural implications of changing? Are people in your congregation supported if they try new things?

INSIDE CONNECTIONS
REFLECTION QUESTIONS

1. How are worshipers involved in your congregation? What are the small group activities? Which activities include faith or biblical study, like Sunday school, church school, prayer, discussion groups, or Bible study groups? In what fellowships or other social group activities does your congregation engage?

2. How many worshipers serve in leadership roles within the congregation? What are the types of leadership roles that are available?

3. Do the worshipers in your congregation feel like they belong? How do you know? Is the trend growing, steady, or declining?

4. Are worshipers developing friendships with others in your congregation?

5. Do worshipers feel there is a connection between leaders and worshipers in the congregation? Do pastors and laity work well together in a spirit of collegial teamwork?

6. Elaborate on the relationship between understanding your congregation's mission (purpose) and the level of participation of the total membership.

Chapter Four

Power Connections outside the Congregation

Praises to God
On mah journey now,
Well I wouldn't take nothin' for mah journey now!
Praises to God —
One day I was walking along,
Well de elements opened up an' de love come down —
Praises to God!
I went to de valley an' I didn't go to stay,
Well, my soul got happy an' I stayed all day!
Praises to God!
Praises to God!

— Aminah Robinson[42]

Serving outside the walls of the congregation to do ministry has always been a pattern in black congregational life. African American religiosity was institutionally created during the slave period in settings beyond the plantation and European American churches. The needs of the community beyond the walls of congregational life have been and continue to be so great that *not* reaching out to others never was and cannot be an option. Black clergy and laity have historically integrated the journey inward and the journey outward in their personal and communal lives. Historically, the black church has been the central institution of the black community. It has attempted to provide spiritual sustenance within its walls, as well as food and other services beyond its doors. This connectedness with the larger black community has very few parallels in American society. Taking care of their own was a necessary presupposition in African American religious life.

This chapter explores worshipers' activities outside the congregation and looks at how these connections relate to one another. It will examine how worshipers invite others into their congregations, contribute to their congregations' outreach or evangelism efforts, and get involved in community service, social justice, and advocacy activities. It will also examine the role that welcoming new members plays within congregations, the different faith backgrounds typical of new people, and the role of a physical community in connecting people to a congregation and its mission. Additionally, this chapter presents a framework of collaboration for congregations seeking to expand their outreach.

BIBLICAL FOUNDATION

For you were called to freedom, brothers and sisters; only do not use your freedom as an opportunity for self-indulgence, but through love serve one another. For the whole law is summed up in a single commandment, "You shall love your neighbor as yourself." — Galatians 5:13–14 NRSV

Because we have seen pain without being moved,
Because we forget your love with solemn pride,
Because we pass by happy before poverty and sadness,
Lord have mercy, Lord have mercy,
Have mercy on us.
For speaking of love without loving our sister or brother,
For speaking of faith without living your word,
Because we live without seeing our personal evil, our sin,
Christ have mercy, Christ have mercy,
Have mercy on us.
For our tranquility in our affluent life,
For our great falseness in preaching about poverty,
For wanting to make excuses for injustice and misery,
Lord have mercy, Lord have mercy,
Have mercy on us.
Amen.
                    — Book of Worship: United Church of Christ[43]

Paul's statement in Galatians 5:14 focuses not on law but on love. Love motivates the ethical life of a Christian. The obligation of the Christian is to embody Christ's exhortation to love one's neighbor as one would oneself. Adhering to this commandment offers us new life in Christ directed by the Spirit.

In early Christianity, sermons were preached in public, but the life of the church was lived in houses. The accounts of Paul accepting hospitality in Christian households and the stories of entire households converting to the new faith correspond to Jesus' commission in Luke 10:5–9, in which he instructed his disciples to go out into the towns. Houses were the basic cells of the growing church, and the hosts of Christian house churches were expected to provide elaborate banquets for the congregants. These groups were socially inclusive, comprising slaves and freeborn persons, men and women.

By the second century, Christians were active in Antioch, Asia Minor, Macedonia, Rome, and Alexandria. By the time Constantine gave official recognition to Christianity in 312 CE, the Christian church had entered into a new phase of its history. Gatherings no longer took place exclusively in house churches but in urban areas throughout north Africa, Asia Minor, and the Roman Empire. During this period the growing Christian community began to determine which writings were approved by the religious leaders and the Christian community. By the third century CE, the Christian Bible had been created. The adoption of a holy text was one of the signs that the religion was crystallizing into the full-fledged belief system that we know as Christianity. Given the rich interplay of religious movements, rituals, belief systems, and customs within the Roman Empire at that time, why did the Christians win out? This new religion had some inherent advantages:

+ Because of its monotheistic roots, it was universal in scope.

+ The God-human persona of Jesus presented a theme very familiar to the Greco-Roman world.

+ From the third century onward, Christianity took on themes from the Platonic tradition, which made the faith appealing to the educated.

+ The nature of its "mystery," a sacred meal, coupled with a scheme of initiation (baptism) made it more appealing than other popular mystery cults of the time.

+ Periodic persecution of the Jews reinforced the solidarity of the group.

+ The emptiness of the emperor cult made Christianity much more appealing. Then Constantine I (d. 337) made Christianity an official teaching.

+ The new religion had consistent organizational practices.

+ Christianity presented a positive, and therefore attractive, outlook towards the world.[44]

A positive attitude toward the world is a core Christian value to this day. It is in part what drives congregations to take that love of neighbor outside the walls of the church. An elemental bond of group identity is forged by membership in a religious community. For African Americans the church has long been a sanctuary. Social conditions placed a special burden on black churches; they had to serve as social centers, political forums, schoolhouses, mutual aid societies, refuges from racism and violence, as well as places of worship.[45]

The religious worldview of African Americans draws from a heritage that envisaged the whole universe as sacred, and it also stems from their conversion to Christianity during slavery and its aftermath.[46] The black church birthed and nurtured such core values of black culture as freedom, justice, equality, pride in its African heritage, and racial parity. The black sacred cosmos upheld and legitimized these values. As we've mentioned before, the spiritual, historical, cultural, and civic nexus of African American life, the African American church is viewed as the single most important institution in the Black community.

BETTY

Born and raised in the church, Betty is a wife, the mother of two, and a student working to attain her master's degree in psychology. Despite her busy schedule, she continues to devote her life to helping others. She works in the counseling ministry of the church as well as with the food pantry.

"I find that in helping others, I'm also helping myself," she says. "I find it empowering to be able to give of myself for the sake of others. People ask me if I feel like I'm giving away too much time, energy, effort, and money to people who sometimes don't even appreciate it, but I tell them that it's not only the people I work with who get help with problems or issues they may be having, but I also receive a great deal of benefit from my experiences with them. I don't want to be a hypocrite. How can I tell others they should be doing this or that, and I'm not taking my own advice? It's important for me to practice what I preach!"

For many, helping others brings much joy. They not only discover things about others, but also about themselves. Issues they might have, hurts they might have been concealing — these are things one can learn about oneself just by talking to others. Betty tries not to let her own issues become part of these conversations, although when she has time to reflect, she allows herself to examine themes that might have arisen that she needs to address in her own life.

As an orphan growing up, Betty moved around a lot, so she knows what it's like to do without. At a young age, she became sensitive to those who fell on hard times and needed some assistance during those times. "I feel a sense of obligation to them, not only because I know where they are and how they feel, but also because of the blessings God has afforded me to have in later life—a wonderful family and a wonderful career.

"I am also very aware not to make people feel ashamed about needing help. I try not to take away their dignity or pride when I'm helping them. I get a great sense of satisfaction and fulfillment when I am able to be of service. I feel it's not only what we are called to do as Christians, but what we are called to do as human beings."

KEY ELEMENTS OF OUTSIDE CONNECTIONS

How do congregations connect to the community and to nonmembers? Outside connections can be formed through inviting others to attend church, caring for neighbors, and welcoming new people. Although worship is the primary task of congregations, church life also provides a vast array of alternative approaches to living out the call God has on the life of the members. Utilizing the rubric of awareness, analysis, action, and reflection, the next segment looks at some of the ways modern-day congregations are reaching out to connect with their communities.

Inviting Others

Our Christian faith is built on the premise that everyone has capabilities and gifts. How we as Christians use these gifts determines

Do Worshipers Invite Others?

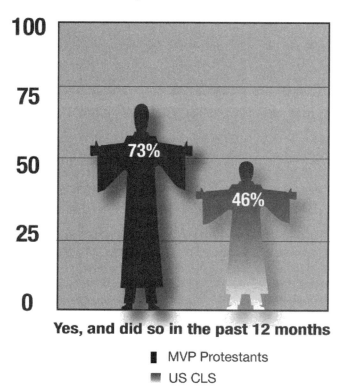

Yes, and did so in the past 12 months

■ MVP Protestants
■ US CLS

Evangelism and inviting others to worship is critical to the existence and growth of congregational life. MVP Protestant worshipers reported that in the past twelve months, 73 percent had invited to their worship services a friend or relative who does not regularly attend their congregations' services. This trend is significantly greater than in the average US CLS congregation, in which 46 percent had asked someone to attend their worship services.

how faithful our Christian life is. How well we encourage and support others to fully utilize their gifts and talents also determines how successful we are in fulfilling our mission and call.

Evangelism and inviting others to worship and participate in the activities of the congregation is critical to the existence and growth of congregational life in many black congregations. This is reflected in the high number of people within black congregations who invite their friends to worship and participation in their congregational activities. Within the black culture, active community outreach is a strong component. Each time a person uses his or her abilities to serve or to reach out to the community, the community is stronger and the person more powerful for having demonstrated usefulness. That is why strong communities are basically places where the abilities of local residents are identified and used. Weak communities fail to mobilize the skills, abilities, and talents of their residents. For the African American community in the United States, the black church is the oldest and most stable infrastructure. Historically, the black church has been, and still is, the place where important issues concerning the African American community are addressed.

Congregations committed to building strong communities focus on empowering people to be useful, as reflected in the common practice of inviting others to church and participation in the congregation's community outreach ministries. Within the black community there are customs and institutions that constantly tap into local talent and abilities. Two examples are neighbors having a tradition of trading their skills and local congregations combining their construction skills to build a community center.

There are two significant shared characteristics of each of these efforts. First, a local congregation acted as a *connector*. Second, the local congregation took people as they were and mobilized them. Can you name two important tasks of community building in which your congregations can be involved?

The raw materials for community building are the skills and knowledge of its individual members, which some communities fail to understand. One reason this vital resource is underdeveloped in weak communities is that the community has come to focus largely on the deficiencies rather than the capacities of its members. Some people seem to be without any gifts or abilities. They appear to be like an empty glass, and so they get called names — ex-convict, mentally retarded, frail senior citizen, illiterate, gang member — labels that focus attention on deficiencies.

One effect of these labels is that they keep many communities from seeing the gifts of people who have been thus labeled. Therefore, these people often get pushed to the outskirts of community life or may even be sent outside of the community to receive rehabilitation or welfare services. Weak communities are full of people who have been pushed to the edge or exiled to institutions. Often, we say these people "need" help. They are "needy." They have "nothing to contribute." The label tells us so. For black congregations, inviting others often includes a fundamental issue: Our core Christian beliefs support the understanding that we each have gifts and abilities.

Youth Programs: A Special Aspect of Inviting Others

Churches demonstrate a high interest and investment in youth programs. Most churches believe that youth can be essential contributors to the well-being and vitality of the community, but often they do not have programs that effectively connect young people with other youth and with adults. Projects that connect youth with their communities are now seen to be the foundations upon which healthy communities and congregations can be built. Many black congregations recognize the urgent need for black youth to have a place to contribute to their community, but for the potential contributions of youth to be realized, the youth can no longer be regulated to the margins of community life.

The unique energy and creativity of youth are often denied in the community because the young people of the neighborhood are all too often evaluated only by their lack of maturity and practical life experience. Given the right opportunities, however, youth can always make a significant contribution to the development of the communities in which they live. Projects that will connect young people to their communities will increase their self-esteem and competence while improving the quality of life of community members.

Young people can make a unique contribution to the development of the community. Usually, they have a certain amount of free time, unlike adult residents who must work for a living; youth often have time during the week, on weekends, and on long summer vacations when school is not in session. This time is an asset that young people can fill with participation in constructive community projects.

In most cases, young people spend much of their free time at home and are confined throughout the week to the neighborhoods in which they live. Thus, they have high stakes in the well-being of the community and more day-to-day knowledge of what actually goes on there. Many young people yearn to contribute meaningfully to their community and can be seen to flourish when they are given the opportunity to do so. Even when youth have become marginalized from the more positive aspects of community life, they still generally remain well connected with one another. Gangs (and gang activities) are clear examples of the immense amount of potential generated by peer groups that is wasted because it is misdirected. When youth become connected in a positive manner with the communities in which they live, they can become effective mobilizers of one another, and, en masse, powerful agents of community revitalization.

Most young people are connected to their families. In families in which the parent(s) have become isolated from community life, young people can effectively mobilize their parents into getting more involved in the life of the community. Although most young people are still students, they can also be teachers and role models. Youth are often the most effective teachers and role models for other youth.

Since they have not yet experienced as many failures and disappointments as adults, young people usually possess a unique willingness to try to solve old problems and create new opportunities. This fresh perspective and optimism are qualities that can make a young person an ideal entrepreneur.[47]

Social Capital: A Power Connection Reaching outside the Congregation

People of faith look for ways to make sense of their lives and to express their Christian faith through mission and ministry. More importantly, people who lead black congregations — pastors and lay leaders — think about their communities seriously. For many black congregations, faith-driven community building is a necessity, although it has limits. Faith-driven strategies are more likely to work than many others that have been proposed, however, because the others have very little prospect of being implemented. Why? Faith-driven community building responds to community needs rather than managing or replicating local initiatives. Our Christian faith calls us to model community building that is inclusive and boundaryless. Our African American experience gives a unique and powerful vantage point from which to do so.

Even the most optimistic of observers tends to agree that cities in the United States have problems brought on by years of neglect and deterioration. Crime, racism, sexism, homelessness, inferior public school systems, alcoholism and drug abuse, gangs and guns, and other social problems are most visible and acute in urban settings, but they also exist in some form in suburban and rural areas. Generally, well-intentioned people respond in two ways to these issues. The first focuses on a community's needs, deficiencies, and problems, and summons large amounts of financial and human resources to address these needs. The second begins with a commitment to discovering a community's abilities and assets — its social capital.

Social capital — which includes broad social networks, the reciprocities that arise from them, and the value of these for achieving mutual goals — has become an influential concept in debating and understanding the modern world.[48] The concept of social capital has resonated across academic disciplines and has moved quickly into the realm of public discourse. There are several suggested reasons for the popularity of the concept of social capital. First is a growing concern to reevaluate meanings behind social relationships and to develop concepts for analysis that reflect the complexity and interrelatedness of the real world. Second, social capital affirms the importance of trust and human networks. Robert Putnam, professor of public policy at Harvard University, is credited with increasing the popularity of the concept of social capital in the United States. Putnam succinctly defines social capital as "features of social life — networks, norms, and trust — that enable participants to act together more effectively to pursue shared objects."[49] In other words, interaction enables people to build communities, to make and uphold commitments to one another, and to knit the social fabric. The concrete experience of social networks engenders a sense of belonging and relationships of trust and tolerance that are highly beneficial.[50]

How, then, can these three "features" — networks, norms, and trust — be applied to civic life as it is experienced in African American Protestant congregations? Few areas of American scholarship have produced as much exciting new work in recent decades as African American studies. An outpouring of learning on slavery, emancipation, late-nineteenth-century race politics, and southern segregation dominated scholarship throughout the 1970s, but as scholars moved forward to explore twentieth-century African American history, the focus has shifted to the examination of black life and culture. This change in scholarly focus paralleled several shifts in interpretation and analysis. Whereas before studies concentrated on physical and institutional structures of black community and the degree to which whites controlled black life, later studies emphasized an "agency model" demonstrating the extent to which slavery and freedom shaped destinies. For example, Gilbert Osofsky,[51] writing in the 1990s on Harlem, and Allan Spear,[52] writing in the 1960s on Chicago, concentrated on the creation of the ghetto and black urban life in general. Current studies, though, reflect a shift back to black southern roots and the black psyche, kinship and communal networks, class and culture, and the importance of church and theology in black communities. Scholars are beginning to recognize the degree to which religious conviction empowered African Americans and moved them to action. The extent to which social and cultural capital are empowering or constraining congregational life and social outreach ministries is of particular focus for an analysis of Members Voices Project data.

As mentioned in the introduction of this book, in 2000 FACT completed the largest survey of congregations ever conducted in the United States, creating a public profile of American congregations. Project 2000, a survey of 1,863 black senior pastors and lay leaders, was a significant component of the FACT study. A key finding for Project 2000 was that outreach ministries receive a major commitment of energy and other resources from congregations throughout the nation, with 85 percent of black congregations providing community service. For black churches, community outreach is as much an expression of faith as participation in prayer groups, liturgical practice, or doctrinal study. The contributions of congregations to the lives of people — in providing them with food, clothing and health care; building homes; revitalizing neighborhoods; and treating addictions (the list could be greatly extended) — are immense.

In the spring of 2003, the Institute for Black Religious Life (IBRL) conducted follow-up research to the Project 2000 study, focusing in particular on the extent to which issues of interest for the black church matched issues identified by the White House's Faith-Based Initiative: at-risk youth, prisoners and their families, elders in need, substance abuse, wealth creation, financial education, church/state separation, the role of fathers, rites of passage, hip-hop music/entertainment, and Afrocentric culture.[53] The purpose of the study was to begin an examination of the role of religion in social and public policy through the eyes of the black church.

Pastors and seminarians from diverse backgrounds representing historically black Protestant denominations (Baptist, American Methodist Episcopal [AME], Christian Methodist Episcopal [CME], Church of God in Christ [COGIC], Disciples of Christ, black UMC, and black Presbyterian Church [USA]) completed the ITC/Social and Public Policy Survey. This survey examined three aspects of involvement and interest in social issues and public policy on the part of the participants' churches: current involvement in social and public policy issues, desired involvement, and sermon topics related to social and public policy. The intent was to identify the predominant social viewpoints of the church leaders participating in the survey. Two hundred pastors and seminarians participated in the survey. The composition of the sample was as follows:

+ Participants were predominantly male (55 percent).

+ Age: 34 percent between thirty and thirty-nine; 28 percent were fifty and older; 22 percent were forty to forty-nine; 16 percent were younger than thirty.

+ Ninety-eight percent of participants were African American, with 2 percent black non-U.S. citizens.

+ Twenty-five percent were Baptist; 15 percent were African Methodist Episcopal. The remaining were evenly distributed amongst Christian Methodist Episcopal, Presbyterian, United Methodist, Church of God in Christ, and Disciples of Christ.

+ States of the home churches represented were predominately southern: Georgia, Texas, Tennessee, Alabama, South Carolina, North Carolina, Louisiana, Mississippi, and Florida. The states represented from the Northeast/Mid-region were New Jersey, New York, and Virginia. Twenty-seven percent of respondents said their home churches were in Georgia.

+ Over 30 percent of the participants stated that their churches were in urban areas, with the next largest group from suburban locations. Less than 10 percent responded that their churches were rural.

+ Thirty-five percent of the respondents were affiliated with congregations with more than 350 members. The remaining churches were small — between 50 and 99 members.

A central theme of religiosity within the black church is spiritual and community outreach. The policy research demonstrated that 68 percent of seminary-trained religious leaders have a strong desire to be involved with faith-based outreach ministries. Of special note was the desired increase of 111 percent for activities related to substance abuse. This is a significant increase in interest from current activities. All respondents also indicated a desired increase in activity for ministries related to social and public policy. Of the six social policy areas surveyed, access to health care had the highest interest (77.7 percent), followed by financial education (75.8 percent), wealth creation (74.8 percent), minority representation (71.2 percent), affirmative action (64.3 percent), and welfare reform (53.9 percent).[54] For the researchers involved in this follow-up study to Project 2000, however, the question became, "What ministries related to social and public policy do the people in the pews want to be involved in?"

When MVP researchers were asked to participate in the U.S. Congregational Life Survey, of particular interest was the inclusion of survey questions related to types of social and public issues. MVP thus included the following question, which had not been included in the original U.S. Congregational Life survey instrument:

In which of the following ministries would you like your congregation to be involved? Mark all that apply:

___ Housing for senior citizen programs or assistance

___ Other senior citizen programs or assistance

___ Prison or jail ministry

___ Counseling or support groups

___ Substance abuse or 12–step recovery programs

___ Day care, pre-school, before or after-school programs

___ Other programs for children or youth

___ Emergency relief or financial assistance

___ Economic development

___ Financial education

___ Health-related programs and activities

___ Activities for unemployed people

___ Political or social justice activities (voter registration, etc.)

On the following page there is a listing of data reported by the more than 13,000 Protestant parishioners to MVP, regarding levels of future participation in social service ministries.

The dearth of quantitative research examining the desire for outreach ministries related to faith-based programs eligible for federal funding is one reason the MVP study sought data to understand the congregational desire for these types of ministries. Additionally, MVP sought data to understand the connections between the types of ministries supported by black Protestant congregations.

Congregations develop a variety of ways to assist people in times of special need, sometimes helping their own members, but often

Desired Social Service Ministries

Counseling or support groups	41%
Health-related programs and activities	36%
Other programs for children or youth	36%
Prison or jail ministry	34%
Activities for unemployed people	33%
Housing for senior citizen programs or assistance	33%
Day care, pre-school, before or after-school programs	32%
Other senior citizen programs or assistance	29%
Political or social justice activities (voter registration, etc.)	26%
Substance abuse or 12–step recovery programs	22%
Emergency relief or financial assistance	22%
Economic development	21%
Financial education	21%

reaching out to help others in their communities.[55] In nearly all categories[56] for data collection in both the MVP and FACT surveys about outreach ministries, percentages of MVP congregations' involvement in social outreach ministries was lower than percentages reported for national averages in the FACT survey. Since the FACT data was gathered from pastors and MVP data is the perspective of the people in the pews, this discrepancy in perceptions of involvement in social outreach ministry is an area requiring additional research.

Another broader sociopolitical context that has particular implications for studying the spiritual dimension of congregational outreach is devolution. Devolution refers to the decentralization of the social safety net and the transfer of social responsibilities to the private sector. It reverses the New Deal welfare policies that emerged from the Depression and which reached their political apex in the 1960s.[57] The proliferation of federal programs during the 1960s and 1970s produced marked expansion of the nonprofit sector.[58] This devolution of government policy was part of a larger reform movement deemed the "new public management."[59] The ideology of this movement was guided by two basic assumptions: (1) the efficiency of markets and the value of competition after a strategy for enhancing organizational performance; and (2) the belief that management styles from the private sector can be applied to nonprofit management. Under the direction of effective leaders, these two trends have generated stronger cooperation between local governments and nonprofit social service organizations.

A foundational assumption of the movement toward devolution is that the impersonal and inflexible nature of government, especially the federal government, renders it incapable of waging an effective war against poverty. A corollary assumption is that private-sector efforts, particularly faith-based ones, are inherently more effective and can mobilize resources with greater efficiency.[60] Examining this assumption is difficult. Empirical research on faith-based nonprofit organizations is limited; anecdotal research is available but difficult to access.

Welcoming New People

A fundamental assumption in Christian churches is that church members are expected to invite and welcome new people. Obviously, churches that receive and retain more members than they lose are churches that are growing — at least numerically. Very few active church members would not know the often highlighted Great Commission recorded in Matthew 28:19: "Go therefore and make disciples of all nations, baptizing them in the name of the Father and of the Son and of the Holy Spirit" (NRSV). Most Christian church leaders, both laity and clergy, would assume that this mandate of Jesus is a priority. As disciples of Christ, we are expected to invite and welcome new people to become disciples.

The Project 2000 national study of black congregations discovered that a strong majority of African American churches (70 percent) reported that they did "very well" or "quite well" in incorporating new persons into their congregational life and fellowship.[61] In comparison to other faith communities, such as liberal, moderate, and evangelical Protestants, as well as Catholic and Orthodox, the historical black churches reported a higher level of incorporation of new members.[62]

Dash and Chapman, in their book *The Shape of Zion: Leadership and Life in Black Churches,* suggest that:

> Congregations welcome new people all the time. These persons are retained, however, as they are nurtured, assisted to learn the congregation's story, become aware of its ethos, and are given opportunities to share their gifts and thus become involved fully in the life of that congregation. Where persons do not have these experiences and are not made to feel welcomed, they cycle out as readily as they cycle into the life of that congregation. Congregational life should provide many opportunities for persons to grow in their faith. They

Worshipers' Length of Time in Current Congregation

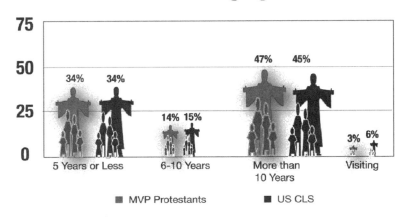

The doors of the church are, indeed, open. Nationally, about 34 percent of all US CLS worshipers report attending their churches for five years or less — identical to the percentage of MVP congregants who have also been members of their congregations for five years or less. However, in MVP congregations, visitors make up only 3 percent of worshipers, compared to the national average of 6 percent who are visitors in US CLS congregations.

should assist persons in their search and exploration into an integrated experience where faith coincides with values.[63]

Prior to the incorporation of new members, however, new people or visitors have to be welcomed when they walk in the doors of a congregation. Those doors have been open, according to our examination of black churches, similar to those in more European American faith communities. Approximately one-third of MVP worshipers and US CLS worshipers report that they have been attending their respective churches for five years or less.

What type of faith background is typical of the new people who become a part of black congregations? New people (those attending a church five years or less) come from essentially four different backgrounds: first-timers, returnees, switchers, and transfers. First-timers represent those individuals who attend a church service or program for the first time. Returnees are persons who have never regularly attended church anywhere or who have come back after not attending any faith community for several years. Switchers are

New Congregants' Origins

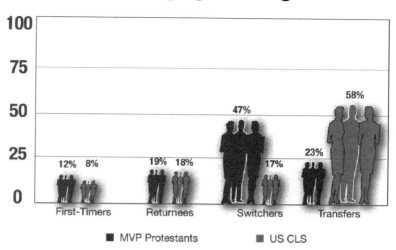

MVP congregations report high levels of new people (those attending five years or less) who are church "switchers," those who have participated in other congregations of different faith traditions, while US CLS congregations have significantly higher levers of church "transfers," those who were participating in another congregation of the same denomination immediately prior to attending their current congregation.

people who have participated in other congregations of different faith traditions, while transfers make up that group of people who are members of the same denominational group immediately prior to joining their current church.

Among the US CLS worshipers, the most significant numbers of people come to a particular church by transfer of membership. They are already a part of a specific denominational group and simply transfer from one local church to another. Fifty-eight percent of the US CLS worshipers indicated they were transfers. This was less the case for MVP worshipers. The African American laity who transferred their membership accounted for 23 percent. Switching from a different faith background, however, was quite significant among MVP worshipers — 47 percent. This is quite interesting in comparison to mostly European American switchers (17 percent).

In the FACT study of forty-one denominations and faith groups, historically black denominations scored the highest (74 percent)

Church's Ability to Assimilate New People

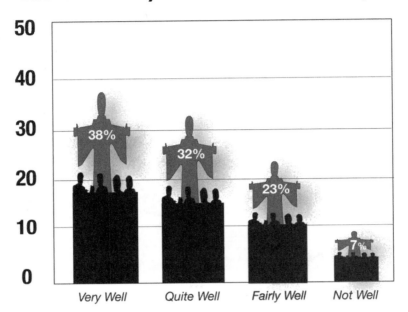

To a large extent, the vitality of congregations rests with how well churches assimilate new worshipers into the life of the church. The strong majority of churches (70 percent) in the total sample of black churches report that they do "very well" or "quite well" in assimilating new persons into their congregational life and fellowship, slightly better than the national average of 63 percent.

among all others in regards to their support for denominational heritage.[64] If one is an African Methodist Episcopal Church member, one is proud of that heritage. If an individual has been a part of the Church of God in Christ, often he or she takes great pride in that faith group's history and traditions. One might easily assume that transferring out of one faith group into another would thus be minimal. In the MVP study of black laity, however, those switching from a different faith tradition represented almost half of all those new people attending within the last five years or less. Loyalty and affirmation of one's denominational heritage, seen in the FACT study, did not match well with the switching of faith groups demonstrated in the MVP study of African American laity. Maybe

Length of Commute to Church

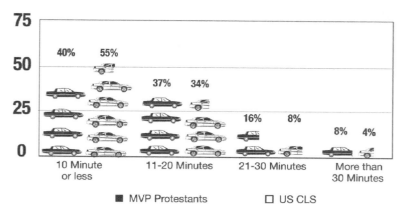

■ MVP Protestants   ☐ US CLS

Time and distance appear to play important roles in church attendance and participation. For the largest percentage of people in participating congregations, it takes ten minutes or less to travel to church services. Most of the people in MVP Protestant congregations (77 percent) travel twenty minutes or less to attend services. Across all U.S. congregations, 89 percent travel twenty minutes or less.

some church members, even though they value their previous denominational heritage, can switch to a different faith community without self-contradiction. Our research in this regard is limited.

Getting Here

Most African Americans (76 percent) travel twenty minutes or less to attend church services with a large proportion of them traveling ten minutes or less. Across all American congregations, 88 percent travel twenty minutes or less. In other words, the majority of Americans are worshiping in or close to the communities in which they live. While this may seem like an obvious fact, it has significant implications regarding the ministries in which a particular congregation will choose to participate. Because most parishioners live in close proximity to their place of worship, they would have access to information that would support building communities through faith connections. Why is this important? It takes the connection between a personal relationship with Jesus Christ and responsible church membership outside the walls of the church in order to build vital links in the development and improvement of the surrounding communities. Religious institutions often have an abundance of resources that can contribute directly to the process of rebuilding communities. How can religious institutions more fully utilize these resources to build better communities? The answer can be found through creating and nurturing a wide range of partnerships with other religious institutions, other associations, organizations, and individuals in the community. These partnerships can unite the resources of local congregations with those that already exist within the community to create a web of social networks that address the most vital issues of the community.

TAKING A DEEPER LOOK AT OUTSIDE CONNECTIONS: COLLABORATION WITH OTHER FAITH GROUPS

Collaboration is a mutually beneficial and well-defined relationship entered into by two or more organizations to achieve results they are more likely to achieve together than alone. Why is collaboration important for congregations wishing to do substantial social service ministry? Collaboration strengthens the connection between a personal relationship with Jesus Christ and commitment to a mission mandated by God. How congregations understand collaborative relationships is reflected in the way a congregation commits to partnerships that help it fulfill its mission. Collaboration enhances black spiritual power.

Collaboration, a more durable and profound relationship than cooperation or coordination, brings separate organizations into a new structure with full commitment to a common mission. Collaboration requires comprehensive planning and well-defined communication channels, and it can be risky because each partner contributes its resources and reputation — thus, to a certain extent, surrendering some power. The results and rewards can be shared, however, and so the payoff is potentially greater. The following is a poignant story of the power of outside connections for a group of black faith organizations to change the lives of teens and their children.

In the late 1980s, Georgia Family and Child Services, responsible for planning and research, became concerned because the state of Georgia was number six in the nation in teen pregnancy.[65] More than seven thousand girls under the age of eighteen give birth in Georgia every year.[66] Georgia also had one of the nation's highest birth rates to teens ages ten to fourteen, and 76 percent of teens who give birth were unmarried — a rate that had doubled in just one generation.[67] Half of all girls who become pregnant as teenagers become pregnant again within two years.[68]

About the same time, the Christian Council of Churches met in Atlanta to discuss issues related to teen pregnancy, including:

• Teen mothers are likely to face a life of poverty: In 1993, 55 percent of women on welfare in Georgia reported having their first child as a teenager.[69]

• Teen mothers are likely to become long-term welfare recipients; 53 percent of the costs of welfare, food stamps, and Medicaid are attributable to households begun by teens.[70]

• Births to teen mothers perpetuate the cycle of dependence: the children of teenage mothers have lower birth weights,[71] are more likely to perform poorly in school,[72] and are at greater risk of being abused than children born to older mothers.[73] The sons of teen mothers are 13 percent more likely to end up in prison than sons born to older mothers; daughters are 22 percent more likely to become teen mothers themselves.[74]

Prior to 1988, social service delivery programs in the state of Georgia that provided care for young mothers and their babies did not provide housing for young mothers and their babies as a family unit. What was their reality? Housing options for teen mothers in Georgia are extremely limited. Prior to 2000 Georgia law required teens under eighteen who receive welfare to live at home or with an adult guardian. For teens whose homes are unsafe or unstable, however, the state offered no publicly funded alternative. The Department of Family and Child Services (DFACS) does not guarantee that teen mothers in foster care can remain with their babies, and in fact, these young families are often split apart when the teen parent is taken into protective custody. Homeless shelters, battered women's shelters, and transitional living facilities usually cannot accept mothers under the age of seventeen. In Georgia, only two homes with a total of fifteen beds served teen mothers under the age of seventeen who could not live with their parents. In early 1997 the beds were full and the state had a waiting list. A national Christian nonprofit organization decided in late 1999 to initiate a program to address this need.

A group home was to be established for homeless mothers who are younger than seventeen years of age and their infants and was to be licensed by the state as a pilot project by the State Department of Human Resources, Office of Regulatory Services, and DFACS. The project provided a therapeutic group home to low-income, socially disadvantaged teen mothers and their infants who were homeless or at risk of becoming homeless. The facility was to provide a safe, structured, nurturing environment where the girls and their babies could experience a quality home life and grow mentally, physically, and spiritually. The goal of the group home was to assist these young mothers in postponing second pregnancies until some of their life goals were fulfilled. Emphasis was placed on completion of high school education or obtaining a GED; acquisition of parenting skills; and development of social skills necessary to make informed, balanced decisions. An advisory board was created to establish the group home.

One member of the advisory board was an associate minister at a large suburban church that wanted to develop a strategic planning component in its mission area. The church was looking for local community development projects with which to be actively involved. The group home advisory board strongly supported this type of involvement. The advisory board member contacted a member of the Missions Committee at the church and asked him to function as the group home board chair. He had substantial financial experience and access to a wide array of skilled managers to assist in getting the project up and running. He agreed to become involved.

The new board chair emerged as the driving force behind solving each of the dilemmas faced by the staff and board for the fledgling group home project. He encouraged and guided the advisory board into developing a strategic plan that included a long-term relationship with the suburban church. The church quickly raised eighty-five thousand dollars to complete the home renovations, furnish the house, and hire appropriate staff for the home. The state had become seriously concerned with the home's financial viability, but because of the significant financial background of the board chair and influx of financial support from the suburban church, licensing was approved. The house opened in August 1999. It has since been honored with numerous best practices awards and has opened a second home for teen mothers and their babies. This home is a significant example of a collaborative effort of several Christian churches, nonprofit organizations, and public- and private-sector organizations. It all began with a church that reached outside the walls of its congregation to address a public need.

In our view, four important characteristics support congregational collaboration with organizations outside the congregation:

1. *Building consensus*. Whenever a group within a congregation or even when the entire congregation decides to begin or build up a ministry to which they feel God has called them to participate, often the biggest barrier to success occurs at the initial stage: building consensus. This stage identifies what problem or ministry issue needs to be addressed. It involves getting individual people to come to consensus about the issue. Issues that can impact consensus building include commitment to the project, parochial views among members, variety of abilities and skills, effectiveness of operation, strategic direction, leadership, and available resources. In order to build consensus, it is necessary to address each of these issues.

2. *Include others from a diversity of cultures, fields, and sectors.* Congregational coalitions that include a wide array of coalition members from other cultures, in both the public and private sectors, generally find that faith is a significant factor and motivation for all the participants in the collaborative effort. Many secular private- and public-sector organizations have reported that the faith factor provided an entrée for their involvement in a collaborative effort with one or more congregations. Secular organizations want to collaborate with faith groups.

3. *Determine what role your congregation would like to play and identify high-level objectives and strategies.* The popularity, and subsequent ambiguity, in the use of collaboration often creates an unexpected dilemma related to understanding coalition processes and outcomes. The popularity of community coalitions that include congregational participation to promote social change and enhance community well-being is illustrated by the number of books that address the topic. Congregation members, however, do not often have a clear understanding of formalized processes involved in collaborative work. Determining what role your congregation would like to play and having clear expectations and understanding of the processes, communication systems, and resources needed for participation in collaborative work in necessary. Deterrents that have impacted secular organizations involved with a faith group include perceptions about collaboration, lack of sophistication regarding strategic planning on the part of faith groups, lack of previous collaboration experience among partners, and lack of organizational capacity of faith organizations.

4. *Demand long-term results.* Congregations that are involved in successful collaborative endeavors outside the walls of the congregation have learned that coalitions have a continuous learning orientation, consistently seek and respond to evaluation, adapt to shifting contextual conditions, dialogue about problems, and most importantly, demand long-term results. In the aforementioned example of the group home for teen mothers and their babies, the focus remained on long-term results; they worked diligently not to be distracted by short-term problems.

Collaboration begins by assembling people, building trust, creating a vision, and agreeing on desired results. Thus, stage one must manage the ups and downs of starting a collaborative effort. The collaboration requires a reliance on each person's integrity, honesty, and fairness, which is why disclosure of the various interests in the emerging relationship is so important.

Besides trust, rituals — repeated actions — are needed. Rituals help us build a common language. They help us feel more comfortable with one other and provide a common ground so that together we can envision our destination and manage the journey. For many of us, the word "ritual" connotes religious ceremonies and shadowy rites far removed from daily life. In reality, our lives are crammed with rituals. For instance, each of us has rituals around personal habits: when we shower, where we squeeze the toothpaste, what side of the bed we sleep on, what we drink while we read the daily newspaper. Our list of daily rituals is actually quite long. What are some rituals in your congregation?

Since ritual plays a significant role in our daily lives, collaborative efforts must acknowledge and integrate them. Because collaboration cannot include everyone's personal rituals, we must create common ones that build shared ownership. In the beginning stage of faith collaboration building, four large tasks are paramount:

1. Bringing people together

2. Enhancing trust

3. Confirming the vision

4. Specifying desired results

Make the Collaboration Work for Everybody

We can create needed rituals by asking group members what they need to feel comfortable. Here's how to proceed:

1. *Ask what rituals are important to each person.* For instance, members might mention starting time, meeting place, availability of food and drink, information management, and so on. Do this in the initial interviews or at the first meeting.

2. *Pool all the requests for rituals.* Then consider which requests best meet the individual needs of the participants while helping to form the group.

3. *Present the rituals to the group.* Build trust by openly discussing the rituals. Decide ways to manage any apparently conflicting rituals.

4. *Distribute copies of the agreed-upon rituals.* Some groups give members special folders for their communications, which in itself is a ritual of managing information.

5. *Periodically review the rituals.* By doing this, we determine which are still valuable and whether to add others.

Any collaboration has its own unique combination of community benefits, yet within the collaboration, each organization also brings its self-interests. The preferences of members within the collaboration — how individuals prefer to get the work done — are reflected in the way a congregation prioritizes the work.

Each congregation is guided by theological tenets that underpin the mission and ministry of the congregation. These tenets determine how a particular congregation acts. Acceptance and acknowledgment of different customs build the trust essential to effective collaboration. Identifying your congregation's strengths will help members understand how to do God's work in the world.

Understanding the role of power and how to use it intentionally will be in the best interest of the community and your congregation. Power is always present and is never equally distributed. Many times some members of the collaboration will have more power than others. In all collaborations, however, acknowledging and appreciating the different types of power each person and organization bring to the joint effort will lead to success. (See Appendix E: Creating Rituals that Support Collaboration.)

Finally, church meetings are notorious for being ineffective. Church members often become discouraged and withdraw their participation from ministries just because of ineffective meetings. For concrete suggestions for conducting effective church meetings, see Appendix F.

This chapter has given an overview of those elements that help a congregation form a community and what the church can do with the power of a community. The final chapter builds on this information by presenting ways for a congregation to enhance its power even further.

GROUP EXERCISES

The following exercises are brief assessment exercises (one to two hours) that Sunday school or fellowship groups can use to begin an examination of outside connections.

Exercise 1: Analyzing the Community Assets of Your Church

This exercise will take you out of the church to investigate your neighborhood's characteristics. Often church members want to engage in ministries that support the neighborhood in which the church is located. Before a ministry is begun, though, a thorough understanding or investigation of the community the ministry is to support needs to be completed. Analyzing and understanding the community assets of your church will help create effective ministries. The process will also help identify collaborative partners for your ministry and will build powerful outside spiritual connections.

1. Investigate the surrounding community:

   ◆ Keep your eyes open: What are the area's demographics? Behavior of people in the community?

   ◆ Survey the building stock, natural systems, infrastructure.

   ◆ Find photographs that speak to the demographics, culture, building stock, natural systems, infrastructure.

   ◆ Professional investigating: Get reports on demographics, culture, politics, behavior, safety, building stock, natural systems, infrastructure, property values.

2. Seek stakeholders:

   ◆ Seek oral histories from people in the community to understand the culture, politics, building stock, natural systems, infrastructure, employment.

   ◆ Develop questionnaires to obtain information regarding demographics, culture, priorities, building stock, employment.

♦ Take an inventory of services in the community that support culture, behavior, safety, priorities, building stock, infrastructure.

3. Use secondary sources:

♦ Read the daily newspaper and keep up with local politics.

♦ Analyze census figures for relevant information on demographics, employment, income and wealth, and property values.

♦ Perform an administrative data analysis of culture, politics, safety, building stock, natural systems, infrastructure, employment, and property values.

Exercise 2: Charting the Assets of Your Church's Community

Make a thorough "capacity inventory" outlining all the various skills and assets for each of the youth, elderly, and disabled persons with whom your congregation is currently working. Assets would include such things as periods of free time, ideas and creativity they have exhibited or possess, connections they have to the community around your church, dreams they have shared, peer groups and networks they are involved in, family relationships, and enthusiasm and energy.

Next, compile an inventory of the key assets and resources of the community as represented by local individuals, associations, organizations, and institutions. When this is done, you will find that these community assets fall into the following categories: a) citizen associations and nonprofit organizations of all types; b) publicly funded institutions, such as hospitals, parks, libraries, and schools; c) the private sector, including small businesses, banks, and local branches of larger corporations; and d) local residents and special-interest groups of labeled people such as "seniors," "the disabled," and "artists."

Use the information that has been obtained from these inventories to identify ways to build strong, concrete, mutually beneficial partnerships among local youth, elderly, and disabled persons and the other individuals, organizations, and associations that exist within the community.

OUTSIDE CONNECTIONS
REFLECTION QUESTIONS

1. How does your congregation invite others to attend worship services? What are some of the important beliefs, religious practices, and rituals that your congregation identifies as distinctive to its denominational heritage and identity?

2. How many worshipers contribute to your congregation's outreach or evangelism efforts? Why do you think your congregation members care about their ministries?

3. In what ways are your congregation members involved in community service, social justice, or advocacy activities?

4. How many new people attend your congregation's worship services?

5. What type of faith background is typical of the new people in your congregation?

6. Do worshipers come from the immediate community, or do they travel in order to attend?

7. In what ways could your congregation collaborate with others in your community to address local needs?

Chapter Five

Continuing the Journey

Nurturing a Powerful Congregation

Therefore, since we are surrounded by so great a cloud of witnesses, let us also lay aside every weight and the sin that clings so closely, and let us run with perseverance the race that is set before us, looking to Jesus the pioneer and the perfecter of our faith, who for the sake of the joy that was set before him endured the cross, disregarding its shame, and is seated at the right hand of the throne of God.

—Hebrews 12:1–2 NRSV

Throughout their history in America, African American religious institutions have been deeply involved in the struggle for empowerment. The previous chapters have outlined the power of God working in the lives of twenty-first-century African American Christians. Black spiritual power has been and continues to be prevalent within the walls of black churches and beyond, expressed in the pulpit and through the activities of the people in the pews. Black pastors and African American parishioners consciously demonstrate their God-given power to contribute to community building, social change, and church development.

The primary purpose of the Members Voice Project (MVP) was to listen to the voices of the people in the pews and to compare, contrast, and better understand how African American churches regard worship, spiritual growth, community outreach, management, and leadership. Four building blocks of congregational vitality were examined in the MVP study and through the first four chapters of this book:

Spiritual connections. Understanding the many ways in which worship and faith are expressed within and throughout the congregations.

119

Identity connections. Identifying the various subgroups within congregations and how members view the future of their faith communities.

Inside connections. Exploring worshipers' activities within the faith community and how these "connections" relate to one another.

Outside connections. Assessing how congregations reach out to serve people in the community.

A unique feature of black spiritual power is the ease with which many members of black churches apply it to both profound personal involvement in their religious communities and at the same time to social and political change. In the black church, personal and public forms of spirituality are one and the same. God's power is celebrated in prayer, worship, and Bible study. God's power is experienced in voting and challenging societal sins in public. Black spiritual power has been and continues to be present in both personal and public conversations and actions.

Retreats are a proven and effective way of empowering people within the congregation. They offer opportunities to listen for the voice of God and receive guidance for decision making, for the congregation as well as for each individual. In the Bible, God gave vision and guidance to enable the spiritual leaders that God had called to fulfill their mandate. Perhaps one of the greatest challenges for Christians in our day is for churches to walk with God so that the world will come to know God through their witness. When a church allows God's presence to be expressed, a watching world will be drawn to God.

This chapter presents a series of guides for congregational retreats based on the Members Voice Project (MVP) model — examination of your congregation's spirituality, identity, and inside and outside connections. The focus is on helping congregations discern God's will for them.

When God wants to reveal God's will to a church, God will begin by speaking to one or more individuals. Because of the nature of God's call and assignment for a congregation, it is often the pastor, though not always, to whom God may first speak. The pastor's job is to bear witness to the church about what he or she senses God is saying. Other members may also express what they sense God is saying. The whole congregational body looks to Christ — the head of the church — for guidance. Christ will guide all the members of the congregation to fully understand God's will for them.

Each congregational retreat is different because each congregation is made up of different kinds of people. The great variety of congregational settings and life experiences of members means that not every retreat design will be appropriate every time or for every congregation. All effective retreats include the following elements: ritual withdrawing from the ordinary, introspection, listening to the voice of God moving within your consciousness, and a conscious return to ordinary life. Silence is one of God's greatest gifts. We cannot hear what God is saying to us if we are always speaking.

At least three distinct kinds of retreats are frequently undertaken: dialogical, personally guided, and private.[75] *Dialogical* retreats rely heavily on the interaction of the participants and are led by experienced retreat directors. *Personally guided* retreats are usually small group retreats guided by one spiritual leader. This type of retreat allows large blocks of time for personal reflection. *Private* retreats often do not have spiritual guides and are used for personal discernment.[76] Persons on these retreats often meet one-on-one with a spiritual director. It is important to choose the retreat type that will most effectively meet your congregation's needs.

BIBLICAL FOUNDATION

We remember that your church was born in wind and fire,
not to sweep us heavenward like a presumptuous tower,
but to guide us down the dust road of this world
so that we may lift up the downcast, heal the broken,
reconcile what is lost, and bring peace amidst unrest.
— Garth House, *Litanies for All Occasions*[77]

A church is a living organism with Christ as the head. All the parts of the body are interconnected and related to Christ. Jesus functions as head of his body (the local church) to guide it in carrying out the will of God. God touches the world through the activities of a church's mission work and even through the everyday work of operating the church. Paul wrote to the church in Corinth: "You are the body of Christ and each one of you is a part of it" (1 Cor. 12:27). Just as your physical body needs every part in order to live a normal and healthy life, so the church needs every member in order to live a normal and healthy church life. We each can understand the will of God for our church when we listen to the whole body express what it is experiencing.

"I am the true vine, and my Father is the vinegrower. He removes every branch in me that bears no fruit. Every branch that bears fruit he prunes to make it bear more fruit. You have already been cleansed by the word that I have spoken to you. Abide in me as I abide in you. Just as the branch cannot bear fruit by itself unless it abides in the vine, Neither can you unless you abide in me. I am the vine and you are the branches. Those who abide in me and I in them bear much fruit, because apart from me you can do nothing. Whoever does not abide in me is thrown away like a branch and withers; Such branches are gathered, thrown into the fire, and burned. If you abide in me, and my words abide in you, ask for whatever you wish, and it will be done for you. My Father is glorified by this, that you bear much fruit and become my disciples. As the Father has loved me, so I have loved you, abide in my love. If you keep my commandments, you will abide in my love, just as I have kept my Father's commandments and abide in his love. I have said these things to you so that my joy may be in you, and that your joy is complete.

"This is my commandment, that you love one another as I have loved you. No one has greater love than this, to lay down one's life for one's friends. You are my friends if you do what I command you. I do not call you servants any longer, because the servant does not know what the master is doing; but I have called you friends, because I have made known to you everything that I have heard from my Father. You did not choose me but I chose you. And I appointed you to go and bear fruit, fruit that will last, so that the Father will give you whatever you ask him in my name." — John 15:1–16 NRSV

This chapter of John's Gospel is precious to Christians. It gives the Christian the secret to a happy and fruitful life at a time when Jesus is still physically separate from us but spiritually within us. When Jesus says in verse 1, "I am the true vine," he employs a type of symbolism that would have been easily understood by the disciples. Many times throughout the Old Testament, God described the people of Israel as a "vine." In fact, the vine became the spiritual symbol of Israel. The vine was engraved on the coins of the Maccabees, and Herod's temple was famous for its golden vine on the door of the temple.

When Jesus speaks of himself as the true vine, he presents himself as being united with his disciples. He is the vine and the disciples are the branches. Together they embody the new humanity bringing forth the fruit of justice on earth for which humankind was created. Jesus compares his relationship with the church to that between the root and trunk of a vine and its branches. He emphasizes that as the branches draw their life and sustenance from the vine, so the disciples should draw all their life and sustenance from Jesus within them. Likewise, the church, as part of the vine, is inseparable from Jesus.

Jesus makes five statements concerning fruit-bearing in verses 2 through 6. In verse 2, God wants branches to bring forth fruit. A gardener prunes fruit-bearing branches by removing obstructions or deadwood to enable them to produce more and bigger fruit. Deadwood diverts the strength of the branch into unnecessary channels. God, our gardener, places us in situations where we can be most fruitful. God also purges us of deadwood that obstructs the fruit of the new nature created in us by the Holy Spirit.

Verse 3 seems related to the symbolic cleansing of John 13:10 which points to Calvary. When the disciples believed in the word of Jesus, God saw them as already "clean." Verse 4 tells us that if we choose to think, feel, make decisions, talk, and work using our human nature as our source of energy, the result will be no fruit — neither the fruit of a Christ-like character expressed in daily life nor the fruit of Jesus being born through our influences in those with whom we interact. Verse 5 tells us that to live abiding in Jesus is to produce much fruit with regard to Christian character and much fruit with regard to influencing others. Jesus gave this divine secret to his disciples. He wanted to deliver them from the futility and hopeless burden of trying to fulfill God's pattern for living and call to service through self-effort alone. If Jesus had not given us this promise of the power of fruitfulness, we would be bound by frustration and a realization of our inadequacy for the task in our secular world.

Jesus gave his disciples several privileges that he promises to the believer whose life is permeated by him and who consciously experiences his power through depending on him. The first is the privilege of answered prayer. God wants us to experience daily the delight and confidence that come from seeing him do something that was otherwise completely impossible. The second is the privilege of consciously glorifying God. To be abiding in Jesus is to have the profound satisfaction of manifesting in one's person and life the grace and greatness of God's character. Psychologists direct individuals to understand their human potential and seek to fulfill it.

There is also a second meaning in Scripture concerning the word "fruit." To bring forth much fruit refers to success in one's life work on behalf of humanity. Jesus promised fruit that is guaranteed to last for eternity to those who abide in him.

The remainder of this chapter discusses approaches to congregational retreats. The purpose of these retreats is to nurture and encourage the building of congregational connections based upon biblical foundations.

CONGREGATIONAL RETREAT PLANS

Three formats are generally most effective for group congregational retreats: long retreats (two days or longer), mini-retreats (one day or less), or shared retreats (using small groups). The type of retreat your congregation chooses will depend upon the goals it sets for the retreat. Congregations that utilize the MVP model for examining their spiritual, identity, inside, and outside connections find that a series of retreats as well as a variety of retreat types addressing particular topics is most effective. The MVP model emphasizes two important perspectives: the importance of hearing multiple voices from the people in the pews, and the importance of understanding what God is calling your particular church to do at this time and in this place. Perhaps one of the greatest challenges for churches today is to walk with God. When a church makes room for God's presence and actions, both the inside community of the church and the community outside the church will be drawn to God. How can your church be that kind of church? The first task is to understand who you are as a congregation in relation to God and to each other.

Below are necessary components for all retreats, no matter what length.

Preparation

Create an *intention* for a congregational retreat. An intention is not a goal, although it may be presented as one. Rather, an intention is an aim that guides action. A goal, by contrast, is the purpose or objective toward which an endeavor is directed. Intention is focused on an unfolding of the Spirit, a listening for the call of God. The word "intention" comes from the Latin root *intendere*, meaning "to stretch toward something." Keep it simple. Hoping for a particular result is fine. Demanding, planning, or expecting one is not. Try to remain open to the mystery of God moving within the life of the congregation. The most important step is calling the congregation to retreat and developing a desire to hear the call of God on the congregation. Expect God to transform the congregation through the retreat — and celebrate the transformation!

In the preparation phase you are sending a signal that this is a serious time apart and you are determining what the focus will be. This phase involves spiritually, mentally, emotionally, and physically preparing congregational members for the retreat as well as organizing the retreat.

Create a planning team

This team will manage the practical aspects of the retreat. They will develop a to-do list, schedule completion dates for various activities, and determine who is responsible for various components. Often, it is part of the planning committee's role to determine the intention of the retreat, who will be participating, the location, and the goals.

Determine the purpose

Determining the intention of the retreat at the beginning of the planning process is an important element for success. You may ask, is the purpose of the retreat to

+ discern God's purpose for the congregation?
+ help congregational members grow spiritually?
+ look at the congregation's identity?
+ look at connections inside the congregation?
+ look at connections outside the congregation?

The intention chosen will impact the planning that will need to be done for the retreat.

Create a schedule

Create a timeline for retreat planning that will include all preparation activities, such as:

+ selecting the site
+ engaging the congregation
+ selecting leadership
+ determining registration procedures
+ setting budgets
+ designing the retreat

Include in the calendar the actual retreat and follow-up evaluation activities.

Plan the retreat

This phase encompasses the details related to the actual retreat event and answers the question, How long will the retreat be?

When you are trying to determine how long you might retreat, consider a series of retreats made up of a wide variety of mini-retreats designed around particular age groups and interests. People in their twenties, thirties, and forties with job and family responsibilities have limited time and opportunities to get away for extended periods of time. People in their fifties and sixties may have more time available. Mini-retreats as short as an hour may also be appropriate for some groups within your congregation as long as they adhere to the archetypal structure of retreat: ritual withdrawing from the ordinary, introspection, listening to the voice of God moving within your consciousness, and a conscious return to ordinary life.

Each age group will also have a different focus. Younger people tend to be more focused on activity. People with more life experience tend to seek a deeper consciousness of who we are and an identity based not on the ego but on the soul. Each group will hear God's call for the congregation differently. Planning retreats that are appropriate to each group will be more effective than planning one retreat for all that tries to get the answer. Hearing God's call on the congregation, fortunately, is a multistep process.

After the dates for the retreat have been selected, create a detailed schedule. Determine when the retreat will begin, times for meals, breaks, and worship periods. Small group and plenary discussion times need to be included and leaders identified for each session. An important component for all retreats is time for reflection.

MVP SUGGESTED FORMATS
LONG RETREAT (TWO DAYS)

Day 1

7:30	Prayer/Walk/ Exercise
8:00	Breakfast
9:00	Opening ritual
9:30	Presentation: Spiritual Connections
	Lecture (20 minutes)
	Small group/plenary discussion (20 minutes)
	Personal reflection (20 minutes)
10:30	Break
11:00	Small group (20 minutes)
	Plenary (40 minutes)
12:00–1:00	Lunch
1:00–2:00	Quiet/Reflection
2:00	Presentation: Identity Connections
	Lecture (20 minutes)
	Small group/plenary discussion (20 minutes)
	Personal reflection (20 minutes)
3:00	Break
3:30–4:30	Small group (20 minutes)
	Plenary (40 minutes)
4:30	Free time or dismissal if this is not an overnight retreat
5:00–7:00	Dinner
7:00	Recreation
9:45	Evening Prayers

Day 2

7:30	Prayer/Walk/ Exercise
8:00	Breakfast
9:00	Opening Ceremony
9:30	Presentation: Inside Connections
	Lecture (20 minutes)
	Small group/plenary discussion (20 minutes)
	Personal reflection (20 minutes)
10:30	Break
11:00	Small group (20 minutes)
	Plenary (40 minutes)
12:00–1:00	Lunch
1:00–2:00	Quiet/Reflection
2:00	Presentation: Outside Connections

	Lecture (20 minutes)
	Small group/plenary discussion (20 minutes)
	Personal reflection (20 minutes)
3:00	Break
3:30–4:30	Small group (20 minutes)
	Plenary (40 minutes)
4:30	Free time or dismiss if this is not an overnight retreat
5:00–7:00	Dinner
7:00	Recreation
9:45	Evening Prayers

MINI-RETREAT (ONE DAY)

8:30	Registration and fellowship
9:00	Opening ritual
9:30	Presentation: Spiritual connections
10:00	Break
10:15	Small group discussions
10:45	Presentation: Identity connections
11:15	Small group discussions
12:00	Lunch
12:45	Presentation: Inside Connections
1:15	Small group discussions
1:45	Break
2:00	Presentation: Outside connections
2:30	Small group discussions
3:15	Break
3:30	Plenary discussion
4:00	Closing

MICRO-MINI RETREAT (ONE DAY)

Micro-mini retreats could be a Sunday school class activity. There would need to be a determination at the beginning of the retreat period of who is willing to engage in the process. A spiritual director for each small subgroup discussion is recommended if more than one Sunday school class participates in the retreat process. The following should be determined before the retreat:

• Start and end times for each session

• Schedule of discussion topics

- Composition of discussion groups (there should generally be no more than two to three persons in a discussion group)
- Each participant's commitment to complete the retreat

10 minutes	Opening prayer/song
15 minutes	Presentation topic (This should be a different speaker each week utilizing the MVP format. The speaker would be someone from within the congregation who is knowledgeable about the particular topic. See topic suggestions in Appendix C.)
15 minutes	Small group discussion (two or three persons in a group)
15 minutes	Large group discussion
5 minutes	Closing

Another way to frame retreat discussions is by discussing the seven dimensions of congregational life. Although these seven concepts also fit well into the four MVP types of connections discussed in this book, they may provide a multidimensional approach that can help provide a framework to examine your congregation with all its historical nuances. This approach looks at seven dimensions of religious practice and beliefs that can provide a richly textured picture of your congregation. Each of these dimensions can be used during retreat discussions or as stand-alone discussions in a Sunday school setting. This multidimensional analysis is meant to give you a description of the movements that have animated your congregation and shaped it.

The first dimension looks at *rituals* that are practiced within your congregation. Every religious tradition has its own practices — for instance, regular worship, preaching, prayers, and so on. They are often known as rituals even though they are often more informal than this word implies. Rituals fulfill a function in developing spiritual awareness and may overlap with the more formal or explicit rites of religion.

- Can you identify rituals that are important within your congregational life?
- Can you put your list of rituals into categories, that is, worship rituals, social rituals, and so on?

The second dimension is the *experiential* or emotional dimension. These are the emotions and experiences that feed the other dimensions. Ritual without feeling is cold, and doctrines that do not provoke awe or compassion are dry. It is important in understanding your congregation to name feelings that are generated within your congregational experiences.

◆ What emotions do members within your congregation feel during worship? What experiences (positive and negative) do members of your congregation have during various congregational activities?

Third, experience is channeled and expressed not only by ritual but also by *stories,* the narrative dimension of religion. All faiths hand down vital stories, and these stories are often tightly integrated into their rituals. In addition to the timeless narratives of the Christian faith, there are important stories within the history of your congregation. Many congregations participating in the MVP retreat format had a sense of a congregational timeline. Members can share their memories and vividly depict what God has called on their congregation to do in the past. Telling these stories helps increase understanding and provides context for the work that God will be calling your congregation to do in the future.

◆ What stories are rooted in your congregational history? What historical events are important to your congregation?

Fourth, underpinning the narrative dimension is the *doctrinal* dimension. In the Christian tradition, we have essential doctrines such as the trinity, salvation by grace, and the deity of Christ. These doctrines are what make the Christian faith distinguishable from all others.

◆ What doctrinal issues can be found within your congregation? What doctrinal issues impact your congregation's interactions with members of your community?

Fifth, while stories and doctrines affect the values of religious traditions, it is through a chosen *worldview* or ethic that the question of salvation is addressed. For Christianity, the central ethical value is love. This springs not just from Jesus' injunction to his followers to love God and their neighbor; it flows also from the story of Christ himself who gave his life out of love for his fellow human beings. It is also rooted in the very idea of the Trinity, for God from all eternity is a fellowship of three persons — Father, Son, and Holy Spirit — kept together by the bond of love. All Christians are part of a community that reflects the life of the Divine Being both as trinity and as suffering servant.

• What ethical values are important within your congregation?

Every religious movement is embodied in a group of people, very often formally organized as a church. The sixth dimension therefore is called the *social aspect* of religion. To understand a faith, we need to see how it works among people. Sometimes the social aspect is identical with society itself, but society interacts with organized religion in different ways. Within Protestantism, there are many denominations with a wide range of governance types. The social dimension of religion includes not only the many people who make up a denomination but also outstanding individuals who are spiritual leaders at all levels of the social fabric of a congregation.

• What social groups can be found within your congregation? What social groups does your congregation interact with at the denominational and community levels?

• Are there gender issues that impact organization, leadership, and activities within your congregation?

The last dimension is the *material* dimension. It includes buildings, works of art, and other material items that are important to your congregation. The material expressions are often highly important for believers because of their connection to the divine, and, as such, are considered sacred.

• What material objects are important to your congregation? What meanings do they have for congregational members?

Our hope is that African American lay church leaders can use retreats and the other ideas in this chapter to help them better understand the strengths of their local church in ministry and mission.

Let us consider how we may spur one another on toward love and good deeds. Let us not give up meeting together, as some are in the habit of doing, but let us encourage one another — and all the more as you see the Day approaching.
                                                   — Hebrews 10:24–25 NRSV

Conclusion

The word "power" can be understood in a plethora of ways. Those of us who are active participants in the church have been exposed to sermons, Bible studies, and other adult learning experiences wherein we have heard and reflected on the meaning of the word "power." We have explored biblical explanations of power — God's power, the power of Jesus, and the power of the Holy Spirit. Some of us have considered the use of power in and beyond the African American community, past and present. The civil rights era was a catalyst for a new and energizing Black Power. For a long time the black church has been closely linked with political power. More than one hundred years ago, W. E. B. DuBois characterized the organized black church as a "curious phenomenon" that blended both family and ritual functions in an all-encompassing way. "So far-reaching are these functions of the church," he concluded, "that its organization is almost political."[78] Elsewhere in the same study, DuBois cast the church first as a social institution, then as a religious institution. Because of their unique position as black institutions, DuBois concluded, "all movements for social betterment are apt to center in the churches," where the "race problem in all its phases is continually being discussed."[79] Economic and political power is still discussed with regularity in both private and public gatherings in black churches, and the black church often uses its moral power and political power to advance the vision and actualization of the reign of God.

Peter Paris, in his book *The Spirituality of African Peoples*, argues that the spirituality of African Americans is related in significant ways to their African ancestors' view of the world and sense of spiritual power. Paris suggests that spirituality

> refers to the animating and integrative power that constitutes the principal frame of meaning for individual and collective experiences. Metaphorically, the spirituality of a people is synonymous with the soul of a people: the integrating center of their power and meaning. In contrast with that of some peoples, however, African spirituality is never disembodied

132

but always integrally connected with the dynamic movement of life. On the one hand, the goal of that movement is the struggle for survival while, on the other hand, it is the union of those forces of life that have the power either to threaten and destroy life, on the one hand, or to preserve and enhance it, on the other hand.[80]

We hold that there is power in the pews of African American churches — a power demonstrated by laywomen and laymen with regularity. Some people of African descent live their lives driven by an internal and external experience of spiritual power. They, like other people, can choose to use that power for the common good or for something less worthy. They can celebrate their God, in their churches and communities, in such a way that others feel the reality of that celebration. They can enjoy worshiping God through the power of the Holy Spirit and share that enjoyment with others in acts of justice and community service. We conclude that this is happening in many black faith communities today; we have attempted to demonstrate that reality in this book. We have used four somewhat distinct lenses through which to view the black church and its powerful people: spiritual connections, identity connections, inside connections, and outside connections. These four components of black congregational life illustrate the key ways some black church folk are connected to God, to others, and to their communities. They are spiritually connected through worship and growth in faith; they are connected to others through shared experiences of identity; they are connected to other church members inside the walls of the congregation; and they are connected to their communities and its people.

We have learned many things from the African American laity who shared their experiences of black congregational life. Some of the important issues we learned about and that are highlighted in this book are:

1. *Spiritual connections* — understanding the many ways in which worship and faith are expressed within and throughout congregations:

   + Seventy-five percent of African American laypeople say they are growing in their faith.

   + Seventy percent of MVP black worshipers proclaim that their worship experiences help their everyday living.

   + A majority (51 percent) of black congregational members prefer music from a variety of cultures.

2. *Identity connections* — identifying the various segments of congregations and how members view the future of their faith communities:

   - Most black churches (54 percent) have small memberships.
   - One in three MVP worshipers (33 percent) is married.
   - Most African American worshipers (72 percent) believe there is a clear vision or direction for the future in their congregation setting.

3. *Inside connections* — exploring worshipers' activities within the faith community and how these connections relate to one another:

   - More than three out of four MVP worshipers (77 percent) are involved in small-group church activities.
   - African American laity (65 percent) have a strong sense of belonging to their faith communities.
   - Black congregants (55 percent) support their churches by tithing.

4. *Outside connections* — assessing how congregations reach out to serve persons in the community:

   - Almost three in four black church members (73 percent) typically invite others to attend worship services.
   - Thirty-five percent of MVP attendees are involved in their congregations' outreach or evangelism efforts.
   - A majority (56 percent) of African American laity take part in service or advocacy activities.
   - Nearly half (47 percent) of MVP church members are "switchers" — those individuals who have participated in other congregations of different faith traditions.

Chapters 1 through 4 sought to demonstrate what active members of African American churches considered important in terms of their connectedness to God, others, and their respective communities. Chapter 5 gave suggestions on how these understandings could be explored in the local church through a retreat format. We assumed that the laity felt empowered by these connections. We held that their way of being spiritually energized (spiritual power), understanding themselves (identity power), staying committed (inside power), and staying involved (outside power) were all part of a greater whole. The ideational and behavioral aspects of their involvement in faith communities were present and accounted for. The majority of laity gave voice to the reality that they were growing in their faith, their church life helped them in their everyday living, they felt hopeful about the future, they had a strong sense of belonging, they were active financial givers, and they were involved in community service. Our assumptions about black congregational life were affirmed.

This book reflects mostly on the ideas, experiences, and actions of women and men who occupy the pews of black congregations (MVP). It highlights the views of these men and women as they do ministry and mission in and beyond their local churches. Our national study of black churches (Project 2000), as seen through the experiences of their pastors, shows some similar realities. A few highlights of that study are:

• The overall view of black pastors or pastors of predominantly black congregations at the beginning of the new millennium is that their congregations are spiritually alive, and that they are excited about the future.

• A majority of pastors feel that their sermons "always" focus on God's love and care (83 percent), personal spiritual growth (74 percent), and practical advice for daily living (66 percent).

• In terms of community activities and other social programs, the pastors interviewed report that their congregations are involved in many such activities. Youth programs (92 percent) and cash assistance to families in need (86 percent) are priorities. About three-quarters are involved in food pantries or soup kitchens (75 percent) and voter registration (76 percent).

• Among all faith communities studied during the year 2000, historically black Protestant churches give the highest priority to community outreach ministries and social justice advocacy.

• More than half (53 percent) of the churches in the total sample of black churches have fewer than 100 regularly participating adult members.[81]

In a word, pastors and laypersons both seem to suggest some of the same perspectives regarding black congregational life. They represented small membership churches. In the Project 2000 (pastors) and MVP (laity) study, the majority of clergy and laypersons worshiped in congregations that had one hundred or fewer active adult members. The vast majority of the laity and pastors indicated that they were excited about the future. The majority of pastoral leaders as well as laypersons confirmed that they were active in community service. The laity (70 percent) articulated that they valued worship experiences that helped them with everyday living. The pastors (66 percent) tried to focus often on sermon topics related to practical advice for daily living. Finally, both the pastors and people in the pews advocated the priority of community outreach and social justice activities. A majority of the clergy and laity hold that opinion. Therefore, some of the implications concerning black congregational life are these:

* Most African American churches are not mega churches but provide stable small membership communities of faith.
* Most black congregations provide a context where the future is not feared but welcomed.
* Most black churches provide a setting that helps men and women to live their daily lives guided by their worshiping community.
* Most African American faith communities provide an environment that affirms the need for and the action in community service.

Other implications could be drawn, but these few affirm again what we assumed about black congregational life. Black religious life in America supports a nexus of connected people, grounded in God's spirit, serving others in and beyond their doors. One of the many ways religious people articulate their view of God is that God is powerful. God is seen as being almighty, omnipotent, all powerful. Other traits are assigned to God. God is loving, all knowing, just, gracious, and merciful, of course, but for the purposes of this book, we have focused on the attribute of God's power. The power of God is the driving force in the process of connecting people in various ways in faith communities. It has been seen and experienced by us as we have observed and participated in black religious life.

Jesus identified himself with the "least of these" in Matthew 25. The text suggests that when we care for and empower the hungry, sick, naked, imprisoned, or the oppressed of the world — we are in right relationship with him. We are given the power to serve others who need us by following the example of Jesus. The Holy Spirit interacts with our religious communities to empower the whole of us, not simply individuals. The Spirit does not overpower, but empowers us with God's presence and mystery, which enables us to serve and be served.

In conclusion, we are part of a faith community that discovers and rediscovers this powerful God, faithful Son and empowering and directing Holy Spirit. Whether we are standing in the pulpit, sitting in the pew, or teaching at a seminary, we are blessed by God as God leads us into God's world for the purpose of justice and peace. Many blessings on all the work your congregations will be doing.

Appendix A

Members Voice Project Research Methodology

The southern part of the United States is heavily populated with African Americans. The so-called Southern Black Belt — Alabama, Arkansas, Florida, Georgia, Louisiana, Mississippi, North Carolina, South Carolina, Tennessee, Texas, and Virginia — has an African American population that far exceeds the national average of 12.3 percent. In fact, there are areas of many states in the Southeast, such as Louisiana, Mississippi, Alabama, Georgia, and South Carolina, where the black population is 25 percent or greater.

It comes as no surprise, then, that more than half of the black churches in the United States are located in the South. African American Christian communities are as strong and vital in this region as in other parts of our nation. This is one of the findings of the Interdenominational Theological Center (ITC) Project 2000, a study of black congregational life in approximately nineteen hundred black churches. Other findings from Project 2000 are as follows:

♦ The overall view of black pastors or pastors of predominantly black congregations was that their faith communities were spiritually alive and that they were excited about the future of their congregation's ministry and mission initiatives.

♦ Most African American churches are heavily involved in a variety of positive social activities and programs.

♦ Twenty-six percent of pastors reported that their sermons always focused on social justice.

♦ The pastors interviewed reported that members of their congregations were involved in many community activities and other social programs, such as: youth programs (92 percent), cash assistance to families in need (86 percent), food pantries or soup kitchens (75 percent), and voter registration (76 percent).

+ A majority (64 percent) of all black clergy interviewed strongly approved of churches expressing their views on day-to-day social and political issues.

+ The most divisive issue among various denominational clergy was the ordination of female pastors. Overall, 40 percent of black clergy strongly approved, while only 27 percent of Baptist clergy and 23 percent of Church of God in Christ clergy strongly approved.

These and other findings revealed many of the important realities of black congregational life at the turn of the century. Project 2000 was funded by the Lilly Endowment and assisted by the Gallup Organization. It used one key source to better understand African American churches: a random sample of 1,863 black pastors interviewed by telephone from February to May 2000.

Interestingly, Project 2000 was a part of a groundbreaking national survey of congregations from Maine to Hawaii called the Faith Communities Today study, in which faith communities of more than forty religious bodies throughout the United States were examined in the year 2000. The Interdenominational Theological Center (ITC) study of black congregations was a significant part of that overall exploration of U.S. religiosity. Roman Catholic, Muslim, Jewish, and Protestant congregations, including historically black churches, were all a part of this study, which was coordinated by the Hartford Institute for Religious Research, Hartford Seminary. The overall study was named Faith Communities Today (FACT). Whereas the FACT study and the ITC Project 2000 study used one primary source, the religious leaders of the faith community, a more recent study, the Members Voice Project (MVP), surveyed the people in the pews to gain a more comprehensive understanding of black congregational life.

Through MVP, the ITC Institute for Black Religious Life (IBRL) in cooperation with the U.S. Congregational Life Survey, focused on the laity of African American congregations. Approximately five hundred communities of faith were surveyed during 2004 and 2005. Four-fifths of those from the approximately five hundred congregations surveyed were active members of black Protestant churches. The remaining one-fifth was either Roman Catholic or Muslim. All three groups — Protestants, Catholics, and Muslims — used a similar questionnaire. The Protestant churches and the Islamic masjids surveyed were both populated by an overwhelming majority of

African American members. The Roman Catholic churches were chosen because of their higher percentages of black laypersons.

The leadership team of the U.S. Congregational Life Survey (US CLS) — Dr. Cynthia Woolever and Deborah Bruce — designed the survey instrument used in the MVP. Their innovative work helped canvas more than two thousand U.S. congregations, encompassing more than three hundred thousand worshipers across a representative sample of denominations and faith groups. The MVP project was directed by the Institute of Black Congregational Life and funded by the Lilly Endowment. Drs. Christine Chapman, Michael I. N. Dash, Marsha Snulligan Haney, Edward L. Smith, and Stephen C. Rasor are codirectors of the IBRL at the ITC. The MVP project director was Stephen C. Rasor, and the full-time project manager was Christine D. Chapman. Dr. James Cavendish of the University of South Florida directed the study of black Roman Catholics, and Dr. Ihsan Bagby of the University of Kentucky led the study of African American Muslims. Cecelia Dixon and Melody Berry, staff members of the ITC, assisted with the project. Denise Blake of SuccesSolutions also helped in the MVP endeavor.

RESEARCH METHODS

While Project 2000 focused on the religious leaders of congregations, the MVP study sought the opinions of lay members from approximately five hundred bodies of faith. The research plan was designed to survey active adult members of black communities of faith in all regions of the United States. This tends to be the most difficult type of social research for many reasons, including complexity, cost, and access. A case study of one or more churches, an analysis of a number of congregations in one location, or even a regional exploration of similar faith groups is certainly less ambitious than working with five hundred religious bodies across the United States. Gaining access to laity in these congregations is even more difficult still.

The U.S. Congregational Life Survey (US CLS) team developed an effective means of working with laypersons in a diverse group of congregations; the MVP leadership decided to build on their methods and analysis. The US CLS had worked with 100 Catholic, 180 mainline Protestant, and 129 conservative Protestant faith groups, nine of which represented historically black Protestant denominations. They had also studied Buddhist, Jewish, and other non-Christian faith bodies.

US CLS found that their project significantly underrepresented black religious communities. This was a key concern for the US CLS team and a significant opportunity for the ITC and its primary social research group, the IBRL. The IBRL leadership knew that the complexity and diversity of black religious communities would make a survey such as the MVP a formidable task, but nonetheless they chose to pursue the project. Although many studies of black faith groups have been completed, a comprehensive survey of large numbers of black churches had not been accomplished until this MVP exploration.

Some scholars of black religion — for instance, Andrew Billingsley in his book *Climbing Jacob's Ladder* — and others have reported that the black church in the United States has approximately seventy-five thousand major faith groups.[82] These include the African Methodist Episcopal (A.M.E.); the African Methodist Episcopal Zion (A.M.E.Z.); the Christian Methodist Episcopal (C.M.E.); the Church of God in Christ (C.O.G.I.C.); the National Baptist Convention of America, Inc.; the National Baptist Convention, USA, Inc.; the Presbyterian Church (U.S.A.); the Progressive National Baptist Convention, Inc.; United Church of God; and the United Methodist Church. The Presbyterian and United Methodist churches, unlike the others mentioned, are made up mostly of European American church members. Both denominations, however, have significant numbers of individual churches with mostly black constituents.

The Project 2000 study of randomly chosen, predominantly black faith communities concluded that approximately half of all black churches were Baptist, 20 percent were C.O.G.I.C., 10 percent were A.M.E, with the other faith groups listed above each accounting for approximately 5 percent or less of the total. When the MVP study was initiated, the percentages of predominately black Roman Catholic and Muslim faith groups were unclear, so it was decided that only fifty of each would be examined in this inaugural membership project. Thus, the research design called for an approximate representation of these various black Protestant bodies among the four hundred examined. The plan was to secure access to approximately two hundred black Baptist congregations, since the ITC Project 2000 study concluded that that percentage (50 percent) adequately represents the universe of all African American faith groups in the United States. Likewise, the research design called for similar approximate representative numbers of churches for the other groups: C.O.G.I.C. (eighty), A.M.E.

(forty), A.M.E.Z. (twenty), C.M.E. (twenty), Black U.M.C. (eleven), Black Presbyterian (four), and other Protestant groups (twenty-five).

Location was also an important consideration in the research design. The ITC Project 2000 study concluded that approximately half of the African American Baptist churches in the United States are located in the South. Twenty percent of the C.O.G.I.C. churches are southern-based also. Therefore, regional considerations were factored into the research methodology. The design also factored in adequate representation of black faith bodies from the Northwest, North Central, and western parts of the United States.

Only four hundred black Protestant churches, fifty Roman Catholic churches, and fifty masjids were selected. There was no attempt at random selection. The ITC Project 2000 study did work with a randomly selected group of approximately nineteen hundred churches, but MVP used a model for selection based on relationships. Since the ITC is a consortium of African American seminaries representing the Baptist, black Methodist, black Presbyterian, Pentecostal, and other faith communities, it was decided that these collegial and denominational relationships would form the database used in the MVP study. Churches were initially selected from general lists of A.M.E., C.M.E., C.O.G.I.C., Baptist, and other denominational groups. Key individuals — faculty, denominational leaders, doctoral and master's of divinity students, and local and regional pastors — were contacted to help with the MVP study. The MVP leadership team had previously established important relationships with these individuals and groups and therefore asked them to assist with the project. They in turn had relationships with alumni of the ITC and other pastors within their denomination. They were asked to provide access to the four hundred black Protestant congregations examined in the study. The specific research design followed by Dr. James Cavendish and Dr. Ihsan Bagby in their exploration of Roman Catholics and Muslims is not included in chapters in this journal.

The survey instrument was adapted from the US CLS original questionnaire. Three different questionnaires were made available to the local black churches: one for the laypersons, a second for the pastor, and a third for the business or church administrator (if applicable). The survey provided to church members had 56 questions, while the ones for pastors and administrators had 105 and 46, respectively. In order to survey their church members, the pastors were provided with a package of materials that included survey

instruments, pencils, instructions for distribution, and other perti-
nent materials. These packages were either personally delivered to
the various churches or mailed. The local church pastor or individual who distributed these returned the completed packages to the
ITC. Most of the pastors of the four hundred African American
churches that participated in the MVP study asked their members
to complete their individual questionnaire at one of the primary
worship services. This was the recommended method used by the
US CLS research leadership team and was successfully adopted by
the MVP program. MVP leadership expected that it would take approximately fifteen minutes to complete the member survey. They
expected that the other two surveys (pastor and church administrator) would probably be completed within thirty minutes, most
likely in a nonworship setting.

In 2004, most of the four hundred black Protestant groups were
contacted about the study. Most of them completed their survey
during 2004. It took much of 2005 for the data to be analyzed and
interpreted. The results of the study were mailed to the individual
congregations along with some suggestions on how to use the information for mission and ministry. The churches received several
reports highlighting their specific strengths, how they compared to
European American and other African American religious bodies,
and how they could use the findings for future work. Several local
and regional conferences were held during 2005 and 2006 to share
some of the key conclusions. Active members who sit in the pews of
local churches and the leaders of those churches had an opportunity
to review and celebrate the various findings of the MVP study.

SOME RESULTS

More than thirteen thousand parishioners in approximately four
hundred African American Protestant congregations in twenty-
seven states and the District of Columbia participated in the
MVP exploration. The study explored four key components or
"connections:" spiritual connections, inside connections, outside
connections, and identity connections. These four groups revealed
a wealth of information regarding the churches' facilities, size,
finances, worship patterns, community services and programs, congregational polities, and outreach. These findings were compared
with the cumulative data provided by the US CLS project. The US
CLS, while diverse in terms of denominational groups, has been less
successful in studying African American churches. The MVP study

focused exclusively on black congregational life. Therefore the US
CLS and MVP data were compared. Many of those findings have
been reflected upon in this book.

In summary, some of the results of the MVP study suggest important discoveries. Black laypersons practice an active faith, valuing
worship and diverse choices of music. They enjoy being members of
small groups and support their faith communities with their financial resources. Black men and women invite people to their churches
and are involved in outreach and service opportunities. The MVP
study suggests that many black congregants are "switchers." Finally,
this early analysis of the four hundred black Protestant churches
suggests that while most of their congregations are small in size,
they claim to have a clear vision or sense of direction for the future ministry and mission of the congregation. They feel positive
about their church membership and thus express a favorable view
of religiosity.

LIMITATIONS AND POSSIBILITIES OF MVP

The rewards of being involved in this kind of study are numerous.
The men and women who sit in the pews in black churches need to
be given an opportunity to join local and national dialogues about
religious life in the United States. This inaugural study of four hundred black communities of faith has given them that opportunity.
Most research conducted in the United States, regardless of which
ethnic or racial group it studies, tends to poll a few key respondents that represent specific groups. Studies of European American
or African American faith communities have almost exclusively re-
lied on a handful of individuals to comment on their communities of
faith. Complexity, cost, and access have been some of the constraints
to pursuing a more comprehensive methodology.

Doing a close study of a few churches is an important method
and often reveals significant in-depth results. Encouraging many
members of a variety of faith communities to share their insights
and collective wisdom, while difficult, is equally significant. The results, however, will always provide somewhat less in-depth findings,
primarily because of the sheer numbers involved.

The MVP study provided an opportunity to hear from the members themselves. It gave the local churches a forum to share their
perceptions regarding their congregational life. This study enables
local congregations, denominational officials, and others to better

understand the spiritual lives of congregations and how they are reaching out to their communities and developing their identities. Hearing from the women and men in the pew helps educational institutions. Educators in colleges, universities, and seminaries need to be aware of the perspectives of the laity in our religious communities. The training of women and men for full- and part-time mission activities and ministry can only be improved when those who provide that training better understand and appreciate the perspective of laypersons in the church. The MVP study helps to provide information for that purpose.

There are limits to any study of this kind. Making generalizations about even a small group of individuals or faith communities is most always complex. To attempt to do so when four hundred or five hundred religious bodies are involved is even more so. Do we know more about these churches having heard from the members, pastors, and in some cases the administrators? The answer would most certainly be yes. Can we now draw universally applicable conclusions of black congregational life in America? Probably not. However, we do know more than we knew before. Much more will need to be revealed through future research projects and studies of African American faith groups in order to draw wider conclusions.

Any project that involves the African American church must take into account that gaining access to pastors and their congregations requires great sensitivity and effective relational skills. The MVP project was not always successful in handling these sensitivities. Thus, access to a broader and more diverse group of churches, both in terms of denomination and location, was somewhat limited. Many of the faculty, students, pastors, and denominational leaders provided access to various churches, and yet some of the goals that drove the project were not completely realized. For instance, a fairly representative group of denominations was pursued. The goal of targeting a variety of churches from all regions of the country was another part of the research design. In the end, while twenty-seven states and the District of Columbia were represented, the South, in particular the state of Georgia, was overrepresented. The northeastern and western parts of the United States were underrepresented.

The actual number of people who successfully completed the membership survey was on average about thirty-five adults within each faith community. The majority of black religious communities are small, with approximately one hundred active members. If the average number of respondents to the MVP study had been closer to fifty, or approximately half of the active members, the results may have been somewhat more representative of those churches that were included.

Finally, when comparing one black faith group to another, or to a group of four hundred or five hundred others, there are significant limitations to consider. The size, location, denomination, context, leadership, political perspective, and other factors would have to be considered before drawing firm conclusions. There are limitations in comparisons between African American and European American churches or faith communities. In the early stages of analysis when the US CLS population of two thousand churches was compared to the MVP group of approximately four hundred churches, many interesting and significant findings were identified. Many of those results are reported in this book. However, it should never be assumed that these comparisons are the final word. The US CLS database had 122,049 members of the laity. The MVP was working with a much smaller number of a little more than 13,000 members. This in no way negates the results but suggests caution when attempting to generalize about either group.

In conclusion, hearing from the women and men who practice active ministry and mission in and beyond the local African American faith community is vital. When pastors, denominational leaders, educators, and students in religious and social contexts hear the voices of active participants in African American congregational life, they will provide more informed leadership in the faith communities and social contexts of our world.

Appendix B

Project 2000 Identity Results

As indicated earlier in this book, Project 2000 represents one of the most comprehensive surveys conducted among black churches in the United States. It involved approximately nineteen hundred pastors in a random sample of African American churches during the spring of 2000. These demographic findings give one of the most accurate pictures of black congregational life in existence.

Distribution of Black Churches by Region

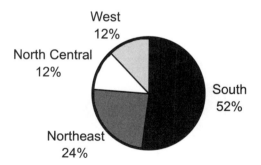

West
12%

North Central
12%

South
52%

Northeast
24%

Distribution of Churches in
Rural-Suburban-Urban Locations

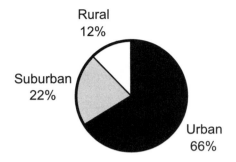

Size of Congregations
among Black Churches

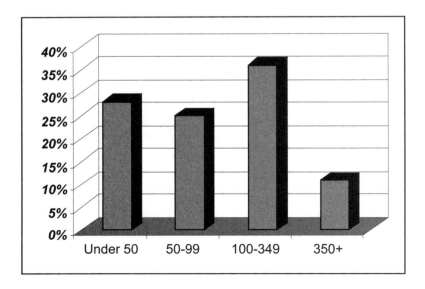

Location of Churches of 100 or More Active Adult Members among Black Churches

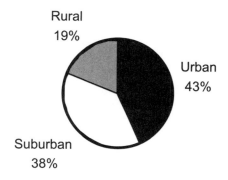

Rural
19%

Urban
43%

Suburban
38%

Year Congregations Organized

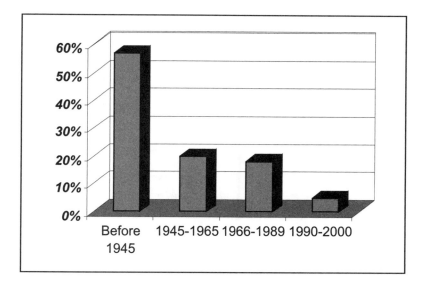

Churches Begun after 1965 by Region

South
18%

West
37%

Northeast
21%

North Central
24%

Characteristics of Actively Participating Adults

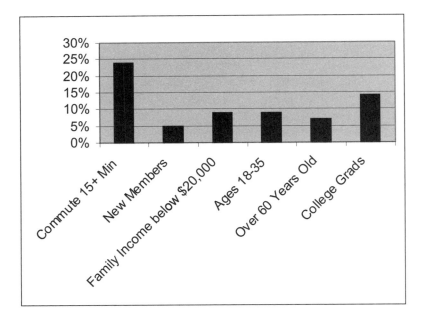

Membership Change in Black Churches since 1995 by Number of Active Members

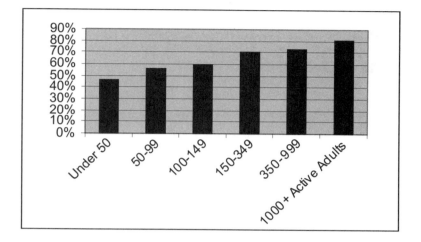

Change in Church Size from 1995 to 2000

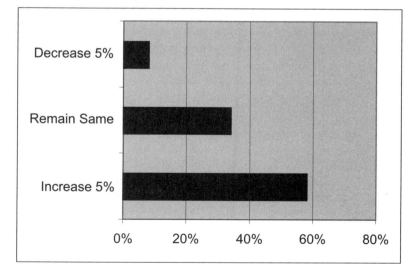

Appendix C

Basic Principles to Remember as a Leader within the Church

1. *Motivating church leadership starts with motivating yourself.* It's amazing how if you hate the job or leadership position you are assuming in your church, it seems like everyone else does, too. If you are very stressed out, it seems like everyone else is, too. Enthusiasm is contagious. If you're enthusiastic about your job, it's much easier for others to be. Also, if you're doing a good job of taking care of yourself and your own job, you'll have a much clearer perspective on how others are doing in theirs.

2. *Always work to align the goals of the church with the goals of volunteers.* Volunteers can be all fired up about their work and be working very hard. If the results of their work don't contribute to the goals of the church, however, then the church is not any better off than if the volunteers were sitting on their hands — maybe worse off! Therefore, it's critical that church leaders know what they want from their volunteers. These preferences should be worded in terms of goals for the church. Identifying the goals for the church is usually done during strategic planning.

3. *The key to supporting the motivation of your church leaders is understanding what motivates each of them.* The key to helping to motivate congregational members to assume leadership within the congregation is to understand what motivates them, and each person is motivated by different things. Whatever steps you take to support the motivation of your church leaders, they should first include finding out what really motivates each of your members. You can find this out by asking them, listening to them, and observing them.

4. *Recognize that supporting volunteer motivation is a process, not a task.* Congregations change all the time, as do people.

Indeed, it is an ongoing process to sustain an environment in which each church leader can strongly motivate themselves as well as congregational members. If you look at sustaining volunteer motivation as an ongoing process, then the process will be fulfilling.

5. *Support leadership motivation by using organizational systems (for example, policies and procedures). Don't just count on good intentions.* Don't just count on cultivating strong interpersonal relationships with volunteers to help motivate them. The nature of these relationships can change greatly, for example, during times of stress. Instead, use reliable procedures to help motivate volunteers.

Preparing for a Congregational Self-Assessment

Congregations need to have a certain degree of readiness to engage in self-assessment. Although there is no set number of variables to assess, you will want to consider some readiness concepts before beginning the process:

1. *Cultural readiness.* Your congregation has a congregational culture in which it is acceptable to provide suggestions for improvement.

2. *Leadership readiness.* Leaders support the self-assessment and the allocation of resources to the process.

3. *Resource readiness.* You are prepared to commit the resources (people, time, money, and technology) needed to conduct the self-assessment. Although the type and amount of resources you will need to undertake the assessment will not be known until you begin, pastor and lay leader commitment to making the necessary resources available is important. Congregational self-assessments require time and typically involve church staff as well as lay leaders. This must be understood and accepted. The assessment can have long-term benefits in terms of ownership and the pace of implementation of change, but these will not be clear at the outset.

4. *Vision and strategy readiness.* The congregation has a sense of where it is going and how it should get there, or has a desire to create a clearer vision.

5. *People readiness.* The congregation has people who will champion the self-assessment process and be willing to work together through a process that may sometimes be ambiguous and will constantly be changing.

6. *Systemic readiness.* The congregation has or wants to have systems in place to provide the information needed to complete the data collection and support the self-assessment.

FACTORS THAT CAN AFFECT READINESS

You Must Have:

* Acceptance of the process by leaders in the congregation
* A champion
* Adequate internal resources (time and people) to do the self-assessment
* A compelling reason for doing the self-assessment

These are mixed blessings:

* Other changes going on at the same time, some of which you cannot control
* A congregation with a history of change
* Past experience with self-evaluations (positive or negative)

It's nice to have:

* Leaders with credibility
* A clear vision in the congregation of where it wants to go
* Additional resources (financial) to conduct the self-assessment

These can be major barriers:

* Past failures and frustrations with self-assessment
* Superficial motives
* Low levels of skills and capabilities
* Negative incentives for self-assessment

Self-assessment takes a commitment of time and energy. It should provide you with knowledge of how to improve the performance of your congregation. It is difficult to estimate how long it should take, however, as the process depends on many variables: the number of strategic issues you wish to explore, the scope of those issues, the type of data you need and their accessibility, availability of staff to be involved in the process, and the type of information you expect to find.

The depth of data collection also depends on the quantity of information needed in order to understand an issue. This may not be obvious at the planning stage. As you begin to collect data on an issue, you may identify the need for more information. The deeper you go, the more you are led to uncover. The process will need to be guided by considerations of time, resources, availability of new data, and the importance of the issue. One of the most critical elements affecting the scope of a self-assessment is the way your assessment team will present its findings to the congregation. It is quite time-consuming, for example, to produce a highly detailed report that links each finding to numerous data sources. This may or may not be necessary.

Understanding your congregation will help you decide on the type of reporting required and the appropriate level of language. If the self-assessment is primarily for internal use, for example, then your report may comprise a set of brief notes, a summary of main lessons, or simply a memo. If, on the other hand, you need to inform external stakeholders of the results, you will need to discuss with them the way they wish to be informed. Remember, you can conduct a thoroughly professional but less formal process to support findings. You and your congregation will need to weigh how much you will or can invest in the process. Some congregations carry out the process in a year; others, with a focus on specific issues for internal use only, complete the assessment in a month.

Finally, specialized activities in the self-assessment can be delegated to produce certain data. For example, a financial analysis can be completed by your congregation's accounting department, which can generate the raw data and the graphics required to interpret the data. Other elements can and should be completed by congregational members.

If your congregation decides to engage in a self-assessment, a number of steps are necessary before carrying out the diagnosis. At this stage, you will probably want to

+ Identify the users of the end results of the assessment.
+ Clarify how the users wish to be informed about the results.
+ Decide who should lead the self-assessment.
+ Decide how much time and effort will be allocated.

The audience for the assessment will influence its scope and the types of results expected. The sooner you identify the final audience, the easier it will be to identify their needs:

• *Inside the organization:* The pastor and lay leaders use the results of congregational assessments to support their efforts in strategic management or congregational change. Lay leaders and staff may use assessment results to improve decisions related to their roles and responsibilities.

• *Outside the organization:* Denominational leaders use congregational assessments to support internal change (learning) efforts, to better identify the effects of their decisions on the congregation, and to better understand their relationship with the congregation.

Once the reasons for conducting a congregational assessment and limits related to the scope of your assessment have been established, take the following steps:

1. Identify clear theological tenets that guide the mission and ministry of the congregation.

2. Identify the theological framework that shapes the thinking, work and life of the congregation.

3. Identify the opportunities and occasions that exist for conversations about God and the congregation.

4. Identify what information you need and why.

After you have clarified the reasons for conducting a congregational assessment and have identified the limits of the assessment, the next step is to identify how you will frame the assessment. Congregations that are conducting self-assessment often begin with an examination of the culture of the congregation and an examination of its resources.

EXAMINING THE CONGREGATIONAL CULTURE

Culture has been described as the common knowledge, language, values, customs, and material objects that are passed from person to person and from one generation to the next in a group or society. Members of your congregation learn about your particular congregational culture through interaction, observation, and imitation in order to participate as members of the group. Thus, your congregational culture drives the actions of individuals that are understandable to the members of your congregation.

How important is understanding your congregational culture in determining how people think and act on a daily basis? Simply stated, understanding your congregational culture is essential for communication with the people in your congregation and the people with whom your congregational wants and needs to interact.

COMPONENTS OF CONGREGATIONAL CULTURE

Even though the specifics of individual congregational cultures vary widely, all congregations have four cultural components: symbols, language, values, and norms. These components contribute to both harmony and strife in the congregation as well as to harmony and strife in society in general.

A *symbol* is anything that meaningfully represents something else. Congregational culture could not exist without symbols because there would be no shared meaning among the people in your congregation. Symbols can simultaneously produce loyalty and animosity, love and hate. They help us communicate ideas such as love or salvation because they express abstract concepts with visible objects. Symbols can be objects that have particular meaning — for example, a cross, rituals, and artifacts.

- What symbols can you identify that are part of your congregational culture?
- How do they affect thoughts and beliefs?

Language is a set of symbols that expresses ideas and enables people to think and communicate with one another. Verbal (spoken) language and nonverbal (written and gestured) language help us describe reality. One of the most important human attributes is the ability to use language to share our experiences, feelings, and knowledge with others. Language allows people to distinguish themselves from outsiders and maintain group boundaries and solidarity. Does language *create* or simply *communicate* reality? If language actually shapes the reality we perceive and experience, then what are the ways in which the language we use in our worship and congregational space affects the members of our congregation? Language is an important means of cultural transmission. Through language, members develop a sense of personal identity in relationship to your congregation. Examining ways of talking within your congregation will reflect your feelings and values.

+ What are the cultural assumptions about men and women that the language of your congregation reflects?
+ Is the language you use in your congregation nonsexist and inclusive?

Values are collective ideas about what is right or wrong, good or bad and desirable or undesirable in a particular congregation. Values do not dictate which behaviors are appropriate and which are not, but they provide the criteria by which we evaluate people, objects, and events. Values typically come in pairs of positive and negative values, such as love or hate, having faith or doubt, being religious or secular. Each congregation generally has shared values that are important to persons in the congregation. When your congregation examines its work and play habits and leadership processes, your core values can be identified.

+ Can you name a core set of values your congregation holds?

Values provide ideals or beliefs about behavior but do not state explicitly how we should behave. Norms, on the other hand, do have specific behavioral expectations. *Norms* are established rules of behavior or standards of conduct. Norms state what behavior is appropriate or inappropriate within your congregation. Not all norms are of equal importance. Formal norms are written down and involve specific punishments for violation. Laws are the most common type of formal norms; they have been codified and may be enforced by sanctions.

Norms considered to be less important are referred to as informal norms — unwritten standards of behavior understood by members of your congregation. When individuals violate informal norms, other people may apply informal sanctions. Informal sanctions are not clearly defined and can be applied by any member of your congregation (such as frowning at someone or making a negative comment or gesture).

+ Can you identify the norms of your congregation?
+ What actions would merit a negative response from members of your congregation?
+ Can you identify the norms of your congregation?

Bringing People Together

Collaboration for Faith Organizations

INVITE A VARIETY OF GROUPS

Successful collaboration means working with every group that can contribute to the vision. Admittedly, the contributions of a variety of groups may be uneven — power is never equally distributed — but each can be vital to success. Our first thought is usually to invite the biggest, oldest, or richest organizations. They can be very helpful, and they are often in the middle of most major activities in the community. But because of this, they are sometimes part of the problem. So choose carefully. Choose those groups that can be part of the solution.

Collaborations start when the members get to know each other and build trust by creating shared rituals. Sometimes you will experience racism, sexism, classism, and unequal power. Hopefully, you will be able to trust people you have avoided in the past. Knowing these difficulties, collaboration first brings the "right" people together. This is a make-or-break item. The challenge of bringing people together requires the emerging collaboration to perform five steps: identifying an initiator, choosing potential members, inviting participation, maintaining the collaboration, and disclosing self-interests.

IDENTIFY AN INITIATOR

All collaborations begin with one or more initiators. They have a vision in mind. They reach out to others, explain the rationale, and recruit group members. Much depends on the initiators' ability to build trust. To do this, they must know themselves and understand their own preferences and powers. The initiators of a collaborative effort have the burden of presenting a shared vision as well as the anticipated results in a way that is defined clearly enough to attract others yet broad enough to include the opinions, skills, and interests of all the group members.

The following anecdote shows how this process works:

A congregational collaborative initiator in a rural part of Georgia wanted to gather people together in a joint effort. As he explained, "I want to make sure that we don't create programs twice for the same people!" He believed the answer to the problem was centralized services. However, as the people worked together, the group realized the issue was access to services. So they built a partnership around educational services leaving the services at their scattered sites. Fortunately, he valued the opinions of his partners in the collaboration.

Power is important here too. Someone with obvious power says, "Let's get going on this." This initiator tends to have a title (pastor, executive director). When this kind of powerful person initiates a meeting, we attend whether or not we believe strongly in the joint effort.

CHOOSING POTENTIAL MEMBERS

Initiators unite an appropriate cross section of people for collaboration. Each person brings something to the table. How do we choose among them so that we have the skills and powers we need? How do we limit our number so that we do not have too much of one thing? How do we make sure that the appropriate grassroots or end-user groups are represented?

We tend to choose people based on whom we know or those who have access to resources, but there are many other helpful qualities. Consider these criteria when choosing potential members:

Capacity. The capacity to sustain effective ministry collaborations varies with the scope of the effort. In one collaboration, five food-bank members in California built a freezer for food preservation. A collaboration in Illinois had ten groups of twelve people working simultaneously to eliminate family violence. This collaboration knew that up to fifteen people is ideal for any one group. Having more than fifteen causes difficulty in scheduling meetings and giving everyone a chance to speak.

Difficulty. Choosing members is an exercise of power because they will later select strategies and control resources. Given this, initiators may avoid people who oppose them or make them uncomfortable. Unusual or difficult partners, however, may be beneficial and necessary to collaboration because they may bring important or different perspectives to the discussion.

Dynamics. Special relationships outside of the collaboration can affect the dynamics of the group. When close friends, partners, spouses, and so on are in the same group, the work of the group is likely to be discussed at other times. This is neither good nor bad, but awareness of existing relationships when choosing members helps one choose the right members for the team.

Familiarity. Shared purpose, expertise, community, clients, and so on will help the collaboration work well (community here means a group united by geography, population, practice, religion, business, or other shared characteristics). A history of positive working relationships that predate the collaboration will help also.

Impact. The proposed members may be the end users (those most directly affected by the joint effort) or people who have access to them. Participation by end users is essential because they know best what they need, and their involvement helps ensure their long-term ownership of the results.

Power. We choose members because they have the power or ability to achieve results. Connections, expertise, resources, position, persuasion, charisma, visibility, and integrity are some examples of power or ability.

Stimulus. Some key people are "queen bees" who attract workers. Given their positions (as pastors, school superintendents, famous personalities, directors of large organizations), queen bees do not have time to remain with the collaboration for long. Their initial presence, however, attracts others who will work hard.

Territory. We tend to invite people from similar disciplines. This is especially true of faith organizations working with other faith organizations, nonprofits with nonprofits, businesses with businesses, and so on. To create diversity, include people from as many different sectors as appropriate.

Variety. Some people are systematic thinkers and have a high tolerance for process; others prefer to implement specifics later on. Collaborations need varied skills and powers. To solicit potential members, you will need to consult key people who know the community and understand the collaboration's objectives.

INVITE PARTICIPATION

Contact a potential member directly or through someone who knows that person. As you make contacts, build trust and support for the mission. To do this, some initiators bring everyone to the table at once to discuss the collaboration. Others meet privately with each potential partner and summarize the private meetings at the first group meetings. Either way, obtain and disclose the following information:

+ Possible community benefits and why they are important.

+ Gains to the participating organizations and individuals.

+ Types of power needed: connections, expertise, resources, position, persuasion, charisma, visibility, and integrity.

+ Commitments being suggested (staff, time, expertise, money).

+ Dates and times for a first or subsequent meeting.

MAINTAIN THE COLLABORATION

An initiator builds trust and creates rituals to unite people. Usually, the initiator of the collaboration becomes its convener. This works when the person enjoys exploring, discovering, and uncovering creativity and potential in themselves and others. But those who initiate collaboration and can spur discovery and creativity may not do as well with bringing the collective vision into focus and attending to detail — and the ability to pay attention to detail is more of what is needed to convene regular meetings of the collaboration. The initiator serves the collaboration best by recognizing his or her strengths and preferences, using them in the service of the group, and admitting to limitations. Most importantly, the effective initiator acknowledges when the time has come to pass the torch to another.

A skilled convener needs good organizing and interpersonal skills, especially the ability to challenge assumptions. Everyone must see her or him as a capable and unbiased person. These skills help the convener establish the trust necessary to reach the group's goals. The convener helps create the routines (rituals) that make the process enjoyable and satisfying. It is critical to select the right person as the convener — someone who can be supportive and flexible, facilitate the group's work, assume authority as negotiated with the group, delegate responsibility, build conditions by which individual members can influence the whole group, all the while retaining some objective distance from the content of what is being discussed and focusing on the process (the vision, the actions of group members, and what is needed to move things forward). A successful convener brings out the best in the participants, so the group can reach its goals.

DISCLOSE SELF-INTERESTS

Building mutual respect, understanding, and trust is crucial in this first stage of collaboration, and is accomplished when we acknowledge how the collaboration serves our self-interests as well as the goals of our home base organizations. To disclose self-interests, discuss the areas important to each person, including customs and preferences. One way to discuss self-interest is for the convener to ask each person to address the following five items, both for what each individual personally needs and what the person believes his or her organization wants:

Culture. Cultural differences, inherent in different ethnic groups, also exist among faith groups, businesses, government, education, and nonprofits. Cultural differences also extend to organizations, professions, and different parts of the country. The collaboration must discuss its cultural expectations and what level of difference is tolerable for the group.

Gain. Each organization and individual represented in the collaboration stands to gain something from being there: money, prestige, contacts, advancement, goodwill, fulfillment of a mission, and so on. A simple question, "Why are you here?" answered by each member from both a personal and organizational perspective goes a long way toward establishing trust.

Diversity. The image of the melting pot no longer portrays American society accurately. Today, people seek acceptance of their differences. For some, diversity is recognition of skin color, ethnic background, or sexual preference. Others consider diversity to be acceptance of their work style, while still others want acknowledgment of how their family situation influences their ability to contribute. Individuals must define diversity; the group must define acceptance.

Perception. The group must work together to come up with joint definitions of how to perceive actions and other aspects of the collaboration. For example, someone may not show up for the meeting. One interpretation is that the person is detained, and the response is "I'm concerned." Another interpretation is that the person is forgetful, and the response is "Not trustworthy." To avoid judgments when dealing with ambiguous terms or situations, we must find common interpretations.

Power. Members need to disclose what power they bring to the group. Some people hesitate to admit to their expertise, wealth, connections, and so on; some refuse to share what they hope to obtain from the power of others. Remember, power is always present and never equally distributed. We must disclose the power that exists and is sought and use group wisdom and convener skills to make sure that we use these powers wisely.

To aid in the disclosure of self-interests, make this point of discussion an official part of a meeting. Document the discussion in a meeting summary, and set specific times to review self-interests at later stages.

Another challenge to creating effective collaboration presents itself in the need to shape our diverse opinions about communal benefits and to separate self-interests into a specific vision. Without a vision statement, separate self-interests can override collaborative interests: I try to get my self-interests met, and you do the same. With a common vision, however, we apply our power and subordinate our self-interests to the larger purpose. A shared vision is essential to enhancing trust. The vision statement tells everyone where you are going. It informs everything you do and generates excitement for all parties.

A vision statement should include the following elements:

* *A description of what we will accomplish, as well as where and for whom we will achieve our vision.* The vision must be an exciting destination worth "going for"; right now, our statement will not include how we will achieve our results.

* *An account of the scope of work.* The vision statement must indicate how big, how many, how much.

* *A statement of unique purpose.* The vision statement must differ from the missions of member organizations.

* *Clarity.* The vision statement must be easy to understand, yet go beyond trite phrases.

Words are important in the vision statement because all the collaborative members and those within their organizations will read them. But since collaboration is an ongoing journey in which you will return to earlier steps with greater know-how and clarity, you need to avoid striving for the perfect words. Spend time on words because they give direction, but not so much time that they limit progress. Strive for consensus; everyone agrees to move forward, even if everyone doesn't accept all the words in the vision statement.

To write a vision statement, brainstorm and list important phrases or words that begin to describe the vision. Then agree on the most important factors and begin to refine the vision statement. Next, ask a subgroup to take responsibility for drafting the statement. At a later meeting, let the entire group modify and ratify the document. Depending on the extent of the comments, the subgroup may need to meet again. In refining the vision, we realize that the discussion — even if it involves conflict — is more important than the statement itself.

Some conflict in wording is inevitable and actually healthy, because the collaboration sorts out values and attaches meaning to phrases the members have tossed around. But beware of conflicts that arise from a perceived threat to some agency or person. If this type of conflict happens, the convener must emphasize that the group is not yet making operational decisions.

Before adopting a vision statement, collaborations usually go through a series of debates. Some groups have taken as long as two years to agree on a vision. If vested interests are deep-seated, then your emerging collaboration should pick up a small, uncontroversial vision, expanding to a more comprehensive vision when you have greater experience. Whatever your statement, begin with something that will lead to success. Here are two examples:

- All youth in our community will have opportunities through education and employment to empower themselves and then to shape their own future.

- Our mission is to expand the role, enhance the status, and increase the ability of women in our community to gain more control over their lives.

Often organizations create both a vision statement and a focus statement. A focus statement is generally a single sentence that captures the intent of the vision and the imagination of the group. Because it is brief, clear, and memorable, the focus statement communicates your purpose to people outside your collaboration more readily than the vision statement. The focus statement often becomes a slogan. Following are two examples:

Vision: All youth in our city will have opportunities through education and employment that will empower them to shape their own future.

Focus: Our youth will be ready for the workplace tomorrow.

Vision: Our mission is to expand the role, enhance the status, and increase the ability of women in our community to gain more control over their lives.

Focus: Women will be equal anywhere and everywhere.

Through writing a focus statement, your collaboration becomes an advertising agency. In this age of the fifteen-second sound bite, you need to communicate essence in an easy-to-grasp phrase. To arrive at this focus, brainstorm phrases and then agree on one phrase that communicates the heart of the vision.

The next challenge is to specify the results you want to achieve. Your vision statement points out where you are headed; your focus statement leads you forward. The statement of desired results is a declaration of the accomplishments you want to make that contribute to the realization of your vision and focus. The more specific the desired results, the better you'll know how you are progressing. The statement of desired results reminds us to stop, look around, and decide if we are succeeding, and continue on the course or correct it if needed. The more specific your desired results, the more you can trust that you will arrive at your destination.

To incorporate the desires of many constituencies and to sustain your collaboration over time, desired results must be long-term. They must also be immediate enough to produce achievements that sustain enthusiasm. These desired results are, of course, related to both community benefits and separate self-interests.

Desired results must be concrete, attainable, and measurable — at least to a degree. That way, your collaboration and your constituents will know *what* you are trying to achieve and *when* your attempt is successful. The words you use must represent positive outcomes, not problem reduction, because when language focuses on problems, problems remain in the forefront. However, when language focuses on achievements, achievements stay uppermost.

Remember that desired results differ for every collaboration. They must be as specific as possible at the start, and be developed more fully as you move along. Clear-cut objectives contribute to a favorable social and political climate in which constituents see your work as cost-effective and as an improvement on current efforts. This sustains excitement about your collaboration and builds support in the greater community.

Those Darn Church Meetings!

Effective meetings are themselves a ritual, marked by such routines as starting and ending times, agendas, or refreshments. They are important throughout the life of the collaboration, especially in the beginning. Initial collaborative meetings are often enjoyable because participants are building relationships, establishing a new context for existing relationships, and exchanging information and ideas, but meetings can go sour when relationships and assumptions are already established or when no one provides valuable new information. Then the group makes no important decisions and the purpose of the meetings becomes ambiguous. To avoid this souring ambiguity, jointly define much-used terms such as trust, respect, effectiveness, or responsibility. The following exercise deals with potential ambiguity. Modify it so that it is appropriate to the culture of your group:

1. State the term. For example: *trust.*

2. Brainstorm specific behaviors that lead group members to conclude there is poor trust. For example: "People are frequently late for meetings."

3. Brainstorm specific behavior that shows average and excellent trust. For example: "People attend meetings, but don't say much" (average trust). "Other people frequently offer new ideas and also listen well to others" (excellent trust).

4. From these lists of behaviors (with negative behaviors inspiring their positive opposites), jointly create a short phrase that defines the term.

When terms are commonly understood, nothing is hidden in ambiguity. Either your meetings are effective (as you have jointly defined effectiveness) or you have something to fix. Different cultures define effective meetings differently. For one group, starting and ending at a preset time might be crucial for an effective meeting. For another group, making sure that everyone leaves with an increased sense of cohesiveness might be a criterion for an effective meeting; for them, ending "on time" is not as important as enhancing the quality of the relationships.

INVOLVE EVERYONE IN THE MEETINGS

The convener must involve everyone by building relationships, taking action, and providing information. Below are ways to accomplish that involvement. Each method must be adjusted so that it is appropriate to the group. For example, one group's action agenda may be a written list of items to be covered, while another group's action agenda may be to eat together and know each other better before discussing business at a future meeting. In either case, shared expectations and open decisions go a long way toward enhancing trust within the group.

Planning

- State the purpose for the meeting(s).
- Issue materials for participants to read or prepare prior to the meeting.
- Create an action agenda by stating the order, lead person, and time allocation for each item.
- Manage the logistics (date, location, start-stop times, refreshments).

Process

- Set initial ground rules for participation and decision-making.
- Begin and end on time.
- Follow the action agenda (but don't stay on a task just to avoid conflict).
- Get the work done that needs to be done.
- Review what has been accomplished (or not) and why.

People

- Acknowledge contribution and participation.
- Build in rewards.
- Carefully manage critical situations and conflict.
- Follow up with those who did not attend.

Paperwork

+ Keep appropriate records.
+ Keep the amount of documentation manageable.
+ Write meeting summaries.
+ Distribute essential information to members and other stake-holders.

Meeting summaries are reports that briefly note who attended, the key issues covered in the meeting, actions taken, who is responsible for each action and by when, all progress, and the main items for the next meeting. Summaries are not minutes, which are a recording of all discussion. Since no one reads minutes, summarize!

EMPHASIZE THE FIRST MEETINGS

Pay special attention to the first few meetings; proceed slowly, and make the agenda for the first meeting clear with established ground rules. (Of course, the group will later develop these ground rules into more lasting structures, roles, and procedures.)

Consider the following questions for the first agenda:

+ Why was the meeting called and who called it?
+ What do people think the collaboration might accomplish? In other words, what are the expected community benefits and individual self-interests?
+ What are the pros and cons of collaboration?
+ Who is not present that might have something to contribute?

Questions to consider for ground rules:

+ What are the roles of the members and the convener, and whom do they represent?
+ What is our timeframe for working?
+ How will we handle information: data gathering, record keeping, confidentiality, publicity?
+ How will communications be managed? In other words, who will see what and at what times?
+ What, if any, compensation will members receive (reimbursement for fees, expenses)?
+ What do we do to get started?
+ How will we make decisions?

Notes

Preface

1. Stephen C. Rasor and Christine D. Chapman, *Members Voice Project Overview* (Atlanta: ITC Press, 2005). See also *The Journal of the Interdenominational Theological Center* 33, nos. 1/2 (Fall 2004/Spring 2005).

2. Christine Chapman, Michael Dash and Stephen Rasor, *ITC Project 2000 Study of Black Churches, Denominational Reports* (Atlanta: ITC Press, 2001). See also *The Journal of the Interdenominational Theological Center* 29, nos. 1/2 (Fall 2000/Spring 2001).

3. Carl S. Dudley and David Roozen, *Faith Communities Today: A Report on Religion in the United States Today* (Hartford, CT: Hartford Institute for Religious Research, Hartford Seminary, 2001).

4. Institute of Church Administration and Management, *A Study on Financing African American Churches: National Survey on Church Giving* (Atlanta: ITC Press, 1988).

5. Christine Chapman, *IBRL Social and Public Policy Survey* (Atlanta: ITC Press, 2003).

6. Cynthia Woolever and Deborah Bruce, *A Field Guide to U.S. Congregations* (Louisville, KY: Westminster John Knox Press, 2002). See also Woolever and Bruce, *Beyond the Ordinary: Ten Strengths of U.S. Congregations* (Louisville, KY: Westminster John Knox Press, 2004).

Introduction

7. Michael I. N. Dash, Jonathan Jackson, and Stephen C. Rasor, *Hidden Wholeness: An African American Spirituality for Individuals and Communities* (Cleveland: United Church Press, 1997), 5–7.

8. W. E. Vine, Merrill F. Unger, and William White Jr., eds., *Vine's Expository Dictionary of Biblical Words* (New York: Thomas Nelson Publishers, 1985), 479.

9. Charles R. McCollough, *Morality of Power: A Notebook on Christian Education for Social Change* (New York: United Church Press, 1977), 11–15.

10. Ibid. 46–48.

Chapter I / Spiritual Power Connections

11. Michael I. N. Dash, Jonathan Jackson, and Stephen C. Rasor, *Hidden Wholeness: An African American Spirituality for Individuals and Communities* (Cleveland: United Church Press, 1997), 104.

12. Ibid., 33.

13. Lorraine Blackmon, Obie Clayton, Norval Glenn, Linda Malone-Colon, and Alex Roberts, *The Consequences of Marriage for African Americans: A Comprehensive Literature Review* (New York: Institute for American Values, 2005), 8–10.

14. J. Mandara and C. B. Murray, "Effects of Parental Marital Status, Income, and Family Functioning on African-American Adolescent Self-Esteem," *Journal of Family Psychology* 14 (2000): 475–90.

15. Roger A. Wojkiewicz, Sara S. McLanahan, and Irwin Garfinkel, "The Growth of Families Headed by Women: 1950–1980." *Demography* 27 (1990): 19–30.

16. Daniel Lichter and Martha Crowley, "Welfare Reform and Child Poverty: Effects of Maternal Employment, Marriage, and Cohabitation," *Social Science Research* 33 (2004): 385–408.

17. Elaine Pinderhughes, "African American Marriage in the 20th Century," *Family Process* 41 (2002): 269–82.

18. R. Taylor, L. M. Chatters, M. B. Tucker, and E. Lewis, "Developments in Research on Black Families: A Decade Review," *Journal of Marriage and the Family* 52 (1990): 993–1014.

19. S. Ruggles, "The Origins of African American Family Structure," *American Sociological Review* 59 (1994): 136–51.

20. Rukmalie Jayakody, Linda Chatters, and Robert Taylor, "Family Support to Single and Married African American Mothers: The Provision of Financial, Emotional, and Child Care Assistance," *Journal of Marriage and the Family* 55 (1997): 261–76.

Chapter 2 / Identity Connections

21. Nancy Ammerman, Jackson Carroll, Carl S. Dudley and William McKinney, *Studying Congregations: A New Handbook* (Nashville: Abingdon Press, 1998), 21.

22. Ibid., 23.

23. Ibid., 21–57.

Chapter 3 / Power Connections inside the Congregation

24. Beverly Wildung Harrison, *Making Connections: Essays in Feminist Social Ethic*, ed. Carol S. Robb (Boston: Beacon Press, 1985), 41. Used by permission.

25. Garth House, *Litanies for All Occasions* (Valley Forge, PA: Judson Press, 1989), 49. Used by permission.

26. Melva Wilson Costen, "African American Worship: Faith Looking Forward," *Journal of the Interdenominational Theological Center* 27, nos. 1/2 (1999): 1.

27. G. T. Hull, P. B. Scott, and B. Smith, eds., *All the Women Are White, All the Blacks Are Men, but Some of Us Are Brave: Black Women's Studies* (New York: Feminist, 1981).

28. J. Dodson and C. T. Gilkes, "Something Within: Social Changes and Collective Endurance in the Sacred World of Black Christian Women," in R. R. Ruether and R. S. Keller, eds., *Women and Religion in America,* vol. 3, *1900–1968* (San Francisco: Harper & Row, 1981).

29. Jacqueline Grant, *White Women's Christ and Black Women's Jesus: Feminist Christology and Womanist Response* (Atlanta: Scholars Press, 1989).

30. W. E. Montgomery, *Under Their Own Vine and Fig Tree: The African American Church in the South, 1865–1900* (Baton Rouge: Louisiana State University Press, 1993).

31. Peter Paris, *The Social Teaching of the Black Churches* (Philadelphia: Fortress Press, 1985), 109.

32. See the works of Evelyn Brooks Higginbottom on Nannie Burroughs and the Women's Convention of the National Baptist Convention, U.S.A., Inc. Also see Evelyn Brooks, "In Politics to Stay: Black Women Leaders and Party Politics in the 1920s," in Louise Tilly and Patricia Gurin, eds., *Women in Twentieth-Century American Politics* (New York: Russell Sage Foundation, 1990).

33. C. Eric Lincoln and Lawrence H, Mamiya, *The Black Church and the African American Experience* (Durham, NC: Duke University Press, 1990), 275.

34. Institute of Church Administration and Management (ICAM), *A Study on Financing African American Churches: National Survey on Church Giving* (Atlanta: ITC Press: 1998), 1–2.

35. Christine Chapman, Michael Dash and Stephen Rasor, *ITC Project 2000 Study of Black Churches* (Atlanta: ITC Press, 2000).

36. Stephen Rasor and Christine Chapman, *Members Voice Project Overview* (Atlanta: ITC Press, 2005).

37. E. D. Carson, "Despite Long History, Black Philanthropy Gets Little Credit as "Self-Help" Tool, *Focus Magazine,* June 1987.

38. Scott Thumma, *Megachurches Today 2000: Summary of Data from the Faith Communities Today 2000 Project*; online: *http://hirr.hartsem.edu/ org/faith_megachurches_FACTsummary.html.*

39. Ibid.

40. ICAM, 94.

41. Ibid., 97.

Chapter 4 / Power Connections outside the Congregation

42. Aminah Robinson, "Praises to God," in *The Teachings: Drawn from African American Spirituals* (Orlando: Harcourt Brace Jovanovich, 1992), 62. By Aminah Brenda Lynn Robinson. Used by permission.

43. Book of Worship: United Church of Christ (New York: United Church of Christ Office for Church Life and Leadership, 1986), 532–33. Used by permission.

44. Ninian Smart, *The World's Religions* (New York: Cambridge University Press, 1989), 246–47.

45. Christine Chapman and Michael Dash, *The Shape of Zion: Leadership and Life in Black Churches* (Cleveland: Pilgrim Press, 2003), 2.

46. C. Eric Lincoln and Lawrence H, Mamiya, *The Black Church and the African American Experience* (Durham, NC: Duke University Press, 1990), 2.

47. John P. Kretzman and John L. McNight, *Building Communities from the Inside Out* (Chicago: ACTA Publications, 1993), 29–40.

48. Tom Schuller, Stephen Baron, and John Field, "Social Capital: A Review and Critique," in *Social Capital: Critical Perspectives* (New York: Oxford University Press, 2000), 1.

49. Robert Putnam, "Who Killed Civic America?" *Prospect* (March 1996): 66–72.

50. Robert Putnam, "Social Capital" and "Civic Involvement," online at *www.infed.org/thinkers/putnam.htm* (accessed May 30, 2007).

51. Gilbert Osofsky, *Harlem: The Making of a Ghetto, Negro New York, 1890–1930*, 2nd ed. (1971; repr. Chicago: Ivan R. Dee Publishers, 1996).

52. Allan Spear, *Black Chicago: The Making of a Negro Ghetto, 1890–1920* (Chicago: University of Chicago Press, 1967).

53. Christine Chapman, "The Black Church: Charitable Choice, Devolution, and Obstacles," *The Journal of the Interdenominational Theological Center* 31 (Fall 2003/Spring 2004).

54. The data generated from the follow-up research for the Spring 2003 White House initiative by the Institute for Black Religious Life have been presented by the writer at the following professional conferences: "Getting a Piece of the Faith-Based Pie," American Sociological Association Section on Sociology of Religion Annual Meeting, Atlanta, August 2003; "Research Report: Black Religious Life in America," NAACP Eighth Annual National Religious Leadership Summit, Atlanta, November 2003.

55. Carl S. Dudley and David Roozen, *Faith Communities Today: A Report on Religion in the United States Today* (Hartford, CT: Hartford Institute for Religious Research, Hartford Seminary, 2001), 46.

56. Employment Related; Substance Abuse; Day Care, Pre- and After-School Activities; Prison Ministry; Elderly Housing; Senior Citizen; Counseling/Hotline; and Cash Assistance.

57. Ram A. Canaan, Robert J. Wineberg, and Stephanie Broddie, *The Newer Deal: Social Work and Religion in Partnership* (New York: Columbia University Press, 1999).

58. Elaine B. Backman and Steven Rathgeb Smith, "Healthy Organizations, Unhealthy Communities?" *Nonprofit Management and Leadership* 10 (2000): 355–73.

59. J. Alexander, "The Impact of Devolution on Nonprofits: A Multi-Phase Study of Social Service Organizations," *Nonprofit Management and Leadership* 10 (1999): 57–70.

60. Heidi Rolland Unruh and Ronald J. Sider, *Saving Souls, Serving Society: Understanding the Faith Factor in Church-Based Social Ministry* (New York: Oxford University Press, 2005), 11.

61. Christine Chapman, Michael Dash, and Stephen Rasor, *ITC Project 2000 Study of Black Churches* (Atlanta: ITC Press, 2000).

62. Dudley and Roozen, *Faith Communities Today*, 32.

63. Michael I. N. Dash and Christine D. Chapman, *The Shape of Zion: Leadership and Life in Black Churches* (Cleveland: Pilgrim Press, 2003), 34–35.

64. Dudley and Roozen, *Faith Communities Today*, 17.

65. Georgia Department of Human Resources, Division of Public Health, Epidemiology and Prevention Branch, "Selected Natality Vital Statistics by Race," 1997.

66. Ibid.

67. *When Teens Have Sex: Issues and Trends, A Kids Count Special Report* (New York: Annie E. Casey Foundation, 1996).

68. Georgia Department of Human Resources Fact Sheet, "Births to Teenagers in Georgia," 1999.

69. Ibid.

70. *The Remaining TANF Recipients: Research-Based Profile* (Athens: University of Georgia School of Social Work, 1999).

71. B. Wolfe and M. Perozek, "Teen Mother's Health and Health Care Use," in R. A. Maynard, ed., *Kids Having Kids: A Robin Hood Foundation Special Report on the Costs of Adolescent Childbearing* (New York: Robin Hood Foundation, 1996).

72. Maynard, *Kids Having Kids*.

73. R. M. George and B. J. Lee, "Abuse and Neglect of Children," in Maynard, *Kids Having Kids*.

74. R. H. Haverman, B. Wolfe, and E. Person, *Children of Early Child-bearers as Young Adults* (Washington, DC: The Urban Institute Press, 1997).

Chapter 5 / Continuing the Journey: Nurturing a Powerful Congregation

75. Rueben P. Job, *Spiritual Life in the Congregation: A Guide for Retreats* (Nashville: Upper Room Books, 1997), 17.

76. Ibid., 17–18.

77. Garth House, *Litanies for All Occasions* (Valley Forge, PA: Judson Press, 1989), 49. Used by permission.

Conclusion

78. W. E. B. DuBois, *The Philadelphia Negro* (Philadelphia: University of Pennsylvania Press, 1899.

79. Ibid.

80. Peter J. Paris, *The Spirituality of African Peoples* (Minneapolis: Fortress Press, 1995), 22.

81. Michael I. N. Dash and Stephen Rasor, "ITC/FaithFactor Project 2000: An Affirmation for the Journey Inward and Outward," *The Journal of the Interdenominational Theological Center* 29, nos. 1/2 (Fall 2000/Spring 2001): 20–22.

Appendix A / Members Voice Project Research Methodology

82. Andrew Billingsley, *Climbing Jacob's Ladder: The Enduring Legacy of African-American Families* (New York: Simon and Schuster, 1992).